Steve Jobs and
Philosophy

Popular Culture and Philosophy® Series Editor: George A. Reisch

For full details of all Popular Culture and Philosophy® books, visit www.opencourtbooks.com.

Popular Culture and Philosophy®

Steve Jobs and Philosophy

For Those Who Think Different

EDITED BY

SHAWN E. KLEIN

OPEN COURT
Chicago

Volume 89 in the series, Popular Culture and Philosophy®, edited by George A. Reisch

To order books from Open Court, call toll-free 1-800-815-2280, or visit our website at www.opencourtbooks.com.

Open Court Publishing Company is a division of Carus Publishing Company, dba Cricket Media.

Copyright © 2015 by Carus Publishing Company, dba Cricket Media

First printing 2015

Printed and bound in the United States of America.

ISBN: 978-0-8126-9889-3

Library of Congress Cataloging-in-Publication Data

Steve Jobs and philosophy : for those who think different / edited by Shawn E. Klein.

    pages cm. — (Popular culture and philosophy ; volume 89)
    Includes bibliographical references and index.
  ISBN 978-0-8126-9889-3 (paperback)1. Business ethics. 2. Entrepreneurship—Moral and ethical aspects. 3. Technological innovations—Moral and ethical aspects. 4. Jobs, Steve, 1955-2011. I. Klein, Shawn.
    HF5387.S719 2015
    650.01—dc23   2015003865

*For my son Sam, whose first movie heroes
were Lightning McQueen and Merida
and who knew how to use an iPhone even
before he could walk or talk*

Contents

Contents

Acknowledgments

I first want to thank David Ramsay Steele at Open Court for coming up with the idea of this book in the first place. I also want to thank all the contributors for putting the time and effort into this project. It is their hard work and ideas that make this book what it is. I merely put the pieces together.

Thank you to The Atlas Society for hosting several Online Research Workshops for some of the chapters included in this volume.

Thank you to the Center for Ethics and Entrepreneurship for its support of my work on this volume.

I also want to thank the crew at the Perryville Starbucks in Rockford, Illinois, for always keeping me amply supplied with espressos.

Lastly, and most importantly, I want to thank my wife, Kristen Klein, for always encouraging and supporting me.

hello.

The Apple IIe was my first computer. As with so many Apple products, the look and feel is what I remember most: the beige, rounded box; the rainbow Apple logo; the feel and sound of the keyboard. It didn't do much, but I liked to fool around with it. I played a few games. I wrote a few school papers on it. Eventually, I started to play around with some BASIC programming. Later, I discovered bulletin boards. It was exciting; it was cool. The Apple IIe would be followed by various Macintoshes and a PowerBook.

But Apple was losing its luster for me. After college, I switched over to a PC. It's what I used at work and Apple no longer differentiated themselves from the PCs enough to justify the price. But with the introduction of the iPod, I returned as an Apple customer. I remember holding the iPhone for the first time. It was so beautiful and cool. I didn't need one, but boy, did I want one.

Apple started as something different than other tech companies. My family didn't need an Apple IIe, but it was too attractive to pass up. The Macintosh was more expensive and less powerful than its typical PC counterparts, but it was beautiful and friendly. But, as the 1980s became the 1990s, Apple had become just another computer company. Computers all looked about the same; they were uninteresting. PCs were as easy to use as Apples. There really was no reason for Apple anymore (and the stock price showed that).

But then came the colorful, egg-shaped iMac. It didn't look like the grey boxes everyone else had. It didn't have a bunch of ugly wires coming out of it. It was beautiful and it was cool. Apple was back. And so was Steve Jobs.

Steve Jobs is one of the most iconic figures of the last fifty years. He revolutionized several of the most important contemporary industries: computers, cell phones, music, movies, and publishing. He represents the prototypical entrepreneur. He came from modest means and education. He was bold and brash. He had an inspiring vision of technology and what we all could do with it. He became fantastically wealthy beyond anyone's wildest dreams.

At the same time, he was known to be petulant, insensitive, and sometimes cruel. He came out of the counterculture of the Sixties and had a long-standing interest in Eastern spirituality. He dabbled in recreational drug use. In these ways, Jobs stands in for a whole range of values and ideas in pluralistic American culture. He was a barefoot billionaire hippy capitalist who changed the world.

Jobs set out to "make a ding in the universe" (*The Apple Revolution*, p. 43). Given how he has done more to change our everyday lives than almost anyone else in the last century, Jobs seems to have succeeded in this goal. Not all the contributors to this book are Apple fans or customers, but we all share an admiration and appreciation of what Steve Jobs accomplished.

Jobs was an outstanding achiever and a complex man with serious faults. This book is neither demonization nor hagiography. It is not intended as indictment or apology. The chapters are thoughtful, mostly philosophical, examinations, from different points of view, of Steve Jobs's life and work, and their impact on our culture and the way we live. Together, they help us to see Steve Jobs in the context of the great adventure of human experience and reflection.

I

The Crazy One

1
The Reality Distortion Field of Steve Jobs

JAMES EDWIN MAHON

It was all a trap, set by a race of beings who could make a man believe he was seeing anything they wished him to see.

—*Star Trek*, "The Cage," 1964

In the *Star Trek* universe, the Talosians are a humanoid race with extremely large heads and diminutive bodies who live on the planet Talos IV. They were once a technologically advanced race, but a nuclear holocaust killed off most of them and left their planet almost uninhabitable.

The few surviving Talosians moved underground and became dependent on their ability to create illusions, for themselves and for others. They became addicted to these illusions, and eventually they lost the ability to repair their own technology. They also began to capture travelers and to use the contents of their minds to create new illusions.

In 2236 the *SS Columbia* crashed on Talos IV. All were killed except a woman, Vina, who was badly injured. Although the Talosians did not know enough about human anatomy to restore her face and body to its original form, and she remained disfigured, they were able to give her the illusion that she was beautiful.

Eighteen years later the Talosians lure the *USS Enterprise* to their planet with a weak fake distress call from the

SS Columbia. A search party led by Captain Christopher Pike beams down on to the planet's surface. They are given the illusion of having found a group of survivors from the *SS Columbia*, including a beautiful young woman survivor, "Vina." Using her as bait, the Talosians kidnap Pike and keep him in a cage underground to determine if he is a suitable specimen for breeding a race of human slaves with the actual Vina. However, Pike resists "Vina" in a number of illusory forms, and he is able to block the mind-reading power of the Talosians with his primitive human emotions.

Pike manages to escape, and reaches the surface. Threatened by the appearance of the Talosians, Pike, with two other crew members, and Vina, prepare to die rather than become slaves. The Talosians decide to let them go, although the humans are the Talosians' last chance for survival. They refuse Pike's offer of opening up diplomatic relations with the Federation in order to get help, telling him "Your race would eventually discover our power of illusion and destroy itself, too."

Vina refuses to leave, because on the ship, away from Talos IV, she would appear as she is, horribly disfigured. Pike realizes that the Talosian illusion is necessary for Vina, and lets her stay. However, the Talosians give Vina the illusion that Pike stays behind to live with her, and they show Pike her illusion. The leader of the Talosians, 'The Keeper', tells Pike: "She has an illusion and you have reality. May you find your way as pleasant" ("The Cage," pilot episode of *Star Trek*, 1964).

Thirteen years later, Pike, now Fleet Captain, is involved in a terrible accident involving delta rays. He is paralyzed and disfigured, and remains confined under medical surveillance in an electric chair at Starbase 11. His former science officer, Spock, kidnaps him and illegally flies him back to Talos IV on the *USS Enterprise*, pursued by Captain Kirk in another vessel. In the course of a trial for court martial, Spock explains what happened to Pike on Talos IV years ago. With Pike's agreement, and Kirk's permission, Pike is beamed down to the planet's surface. The Talosians, who have continued to maintain an illusion for Vina of her being beautiful, create the illusion for Pike (and Vina) of him being physically able and handsome again. Pike and Vina begin the rest of their life together on Talos IV ("The Menagerie," Parts 1 and 2, episodes 16 and 17, Season One of *Star Trek*, 1966).

The Trouble with Tribble

It was an Apple Computer, Inc., software engineer working on the Macintosh computer, Guy L. "Bud" Tribble, who in 1981 said that Steve Jobs was able to create a "reality distortion field" like the Talosians from *Star Trek* (*Steve Jobs*, p. 117). That Tribble was a fan of the classic TV show is not surprising, given that one of the most famous episodes of the show is entitled "The Trouble with Tribbles." He attributed this power to Jobs while trying to explain things to Andy Hertzfeld, a software engineer who came on board the Macintosh project to work with him. Tribble told Hertzfeld everything that the two of them had to do, and showed him the schedule for completing the Macintosh in about ten months' time. Feeling overwhelmed, Hertzfeld said that they couldn't get it done. As he tells the story:

> HERTZFELD: If you know the schedule is off-based, why don't you correct it?

> TRIBBLE: Well, it's Steve. Steve insists that we're shipping in early 1982, and won't accept answers to the contrary. The best way to describe the situation is a term from *Star Trek*. Steve has a reality distortion field.

> HERTZFELD: A what?

> TRIBBLE: A reality distortion field. In his presence, reality is malleable. He can convince anyone of practically anything. It wears off when he is not around, but it makes it hard to have realistic schedules.

> HERTZFELD: What else?

TRIBBLE: Well, just because he tells you that something is awful or great, it doesn't necessarily mean he'll feel that way tomorrow. You have to low-pass filter his input. And then, he's really funny about ideas. If you tell him a new idea, he'll usually tell you that he thinks it's stupid. But then, if he actually likes it, exactly one week later, he'll come back to you and propose your idea to you, as if he thought of it. (*Revolution in the Valley*, p. 24)

About this exchange Herzfeld later wrote:

The reality distortion field was a confounding mélange of a charismatic rhetorical style, an indomitable will, and an eagerness to bend any fact to fit the purpose at hand. If one line of argument failed to persuade, he would deftly switch to another. Sometimes, he would throw you off balance by suddenly adopting your position as his own, without acknowledging that he ever thought differently. Amazingly, the reality distortion field seemed to be effective even if you were acutely aware of it, although the effects would fade after Steve departed.

Reality Distortion Field

Steve Jobs had the ability to convince anyone of anything that he believed. He had the ability to distort your perception of reality, at least while he was in your presence, so that it conformed to his reality. Like the Talosians, he could create a reality distortion field around himself. Although other people might believe that something was impossible (such as finishing an incredibly difficult project in a short amount of time), once Steve got going on them, their perception of reality became distorted, so that they came to believe that the impossible was indeed possible, like he did. As Deb Coleman, one of the early Macintosh team members and a long time Jobs insider, once said: "You did the impossible, because you didn't realize it was impossible" (*Steve Jobs*, p. 119). At least, you didn't believe it was impossible after Jobs was done talking with you—even if you knew that he was exercising his reality distorting power over you.

Jobs's ability to distort people's perception of reality and make them believe what he believed was not limited to employees at Apple. In his keynote presentation speeches at Macworld Expos, Apple Expos, and Worldwide Developers Conferences, colloquially referred to as "Stevenotes," he had the same effect on his audiences. He would get them to abandon all the cynicism that they had, and to believe with him. To quote tech journalist Andrea Dudrow, writing in 2000:

> If you've ever been to a Macworld trade show, or any other event where Steve jobs has been booked to speak, you know all about the so-called Steve Jobs Reality Distortion Field. This field is created around the Apple CEO and is equal in size to the auditorium in which he is speaking. He says things like "insanely great" and "this is really exciting," and you find yourself pumping your fist in the air, hissing "Yesss, yesss!" . . . And then the speech is over and you leave the auditorium and suddenly realize that you just got emotional over an ad for *computers*, that you were up out of your chair screaming and yelling about new s*oftware*, that it was all because this guy, Steve Jobs, made it seem so darned great. ("Notes from the Epicenter")

The effect of such talks on their audiences did linger, even in the face of contrary evidence. As Dudrow adds:

> I remember sitting in a New York City bar late one night trying to shake off the effects of the Reality Distortion Field, listening to a publisher of a Mac-centric technology magazine complain about what a jerk Jobs was. . . . How could this possibly be the same Steve Jobs who I had so recently heard gushing about having the greatest job on the planet? The same Steve Jobs who had moved me to actually get out of my seat and cheer for a measly software revision (and me, a hardened, cynical journalist)?

So powerful was Steve Jobs's ability to make his audience believe what he believed that it inspired a book, *The Presentation*

Secrets of Steve Jobs: How to Be Insanely Great in Front of Any Audience, by Carmine Gallo. It also inspired Scott Adams, the creator of the comic strip *Dilbert*, to draw a Dilbert cartoon in 2010, entitled "Dogbert the Pitchman." In the cartoon, Dilbert constructs a machine that emits a reality distortion field. His talking pet dog, Dogbert, uses it on his audience, and tells them, "Our product is nothing but a block of wood, and yet you need *three* of them."

What Steve Jobs's reality-distorting ability amounted to was the ability to make a completely unreasonable demand, which was nevertheless completely reasonable to him, and to convince people that it was reasonable, or to make a ridiculous claim about a product, which he nevertheless believed, and to convince people that it was true. But was it morally wrong to do this?

The Ethics of Reality Distortion

Scott Adams, the cartoonist behind *Dilbert*, returned to the topic of Jobs's reality distortion field in his blog in 2012, and wrote the following about the depiction of Jobs in Isaacson's best-selling warts-and-all biography, *Steve Jobs*:

> I'm fascinated by the discussion of how Jobs developed what became known as the Reality Distortion Field. . . . One way to look at Jobs's life is that he was a liar and a con man with a gift for design. According to Isaacson's reporting, Jobs had no love for truth. Jobs learned how to lie, cajole, manipulate, and charm until people believed whatever he wanted them to believe. By all accounts, Jobs's mixture of cruel and unsavory skills caused people to produce seemingly impossible results. ("Reality Distortion Field")

Did Steve Jobs do anything morally wrong in distorting people's perception of reality? Adams, following Isaacson, says that Jobs was a liar. It's certainly true that Jobs lied. For example, while Jobs was working for Atari, Inc., in 1976 he got Wozniak (who was employed at Hewlett-Packard at the time) to finish work on the video game *Breakout*. He lied to

Wozniak that Atari had paid them only $750, and he gave him $375. In fact, Atari had paid Jobs $5,000 for the work that Wozniak had done in reducing the number of chips used in the circuit board (*Steve Jobs*, p. 53). Jobs also lied about the computer Apple released in 1983, the Apple Lisa, not being named after his biological daughter, Lisa, born to his ex-girlfriend, Chrisann Brennan (p. 93). And he lied to the authorities that he was not Lisa's father because he was sterile ("The Trouble with Steve Jobs"). Many more examples of Jobs's lies can be found in Walter Isaacson's biography.

However, as bad as Jobs's lies were, there is nothing remarkable about his ability to tell lies. Almost anyone can tell lies. Even Spock lies to Captain Kirk that he has received a subspace transmission from Captain Pike on Starbase 11 in "The Menagerie" episode of *Star Trek*. This is despite the fact that, as Dr. Leonard H. "Bones" McCoy says to Kirk, while they are trying to figure out what has happened, "The simple fact that he's a Vulcan means that he is incapable of telling a lie!" (Kirk's wise response is, "He's also half-human.")

Jobs's ability to tell lies is not what people mean by his ability to distort people's perception of reality. They mean that Jobs could transform their perception of reality, so that they came to believe what they previously did not believe, and to believe what he believed. However, here it's important to distinguish between the power of the Talosians and the power of Steve Jobs.

The Talosians can create illusions, both for themselves and for others. The illusions they create for themselves are such that they *know* that the illusion is an illusion. The illusions they create for others *can* be such that others know that the illusion is an illusion (such as Vina's illusion of being beautiful, and Pike's illusion of being physically able and handsome). In the case of this first kind of illusion, the knowing illusions, those who have them have *agreed* to have them. They prefer them to reality. There's nothing morally wrong with the Talosians creating these consensual illusions, either for themselves or for others.

However, the illusions the Talosians create for others can be such that those who have the illusion *do not know* that the illusion is an illusion (such as Pike's illusion of having found survivors from the *USS Columbia* when he beams down on to the surface of Talos IV). In the case of the second kind of illusion, the unknowing illusions, those who have them have *not agreed* to have them. They are simply deceived.

Non-consensual deception is morally wrong, unless it can be shown to be morally justified. The most common moral justifications for non-consensual deception are benevolence (the deceived person will benefit from the deception), and self-defense or other-defense (the deceived person is attempting to harm [innocent] yourself, or is attempting to harm [innocent] other people). Mere self-interest can never be a moral justification for non-consensual deception. The Talosians deceived the crew of the *USS Enterprise* because they wished to breed a race of human slaves to help them survive. This purely self-interested justification is clearly not sufficient to justify their non-consensual deception of Pike and the rest of the crew, and so it was morally wrong.

There are three ways in which what Steve Jobs did differed from what the Talosians did. First, although the Talosians created illusions for themselves, they knew that they were illusions, and they could always distinguish between them and reality. They did not deceive themselves, in other words. Jobs, however, does seem to have believed at least some of the illusions that he created for himself. For example, after an early diagnosis of pancreatic cancer in October 2003, he refused to have surgery to remove the tumor for nine whole months (*Steve Jobs*, p. 454). By that time, it had grown and spread, making it impossible to remove. At least sometimes, then, Jobs deceived himself.

Second, when the Talosians created illusions for others, either consensual illusions or non-consensual illusions, they knew that they were creating illusions. They knew that they were false. When they created non-consensual illusions for others, they knew that they were deceiving others. However, when Jobs created illusions for others, he seems to have believed at least some (or all?) of these illusions to be true—he did not believe them to be illusions, in other words. If he did not believe them to be illusions, then he was not intending to deceive people. Indeed, at least one way of understanding what Tribble, Herzfeld, and Dudrow are saying is that Jobs was not intentionally deceptive, at least in many cases. He got people to believe what he believed, even though they 'knew' that what he believed was wrong. If he was deceived himself, then he was not being intentionally deceptive, and what he was doing does not stand in need of the same moral justification.

Third, the Talosians always created *illusions*, either for themselves or for others, whether consensual or non-consensual. However, in many cases, the perceptions of 'reality' that Jobs 'distorted' were not, in fact, perceptions of reality at all. Rather, they were what other people *believed* was reality—beliefs about how difficult a task was, how long a job would take, whether something would work, as well as whether or not a product would be life-transforming. What Jobs was able to do was to convince other people to abandon their own beliefs, and instead to believe what he believed—that the task was not too difficult, that the job would not take that long, that the thing would work, and that the product was life-transforming. As a result of changing their beliefs, at least in some cases, people did what they previously believed could not be done. As Coleman put it, "You did the impossible," which of course means that the 'impossible' was not, in fact, impossible.

Indeed, we can understand Jobs as having doing the opposite of what the Talosians did, at least in some cases. Rather than providing people with illusions, Jobs freed them from their illusions. He liberated them from their false beliefs. He ended their deception. We only have to think of the TV commercial that launched the Macintosh in 1984, which depicted people as brainwashed prisoners of "Big Brother" IBM, and the Macintosh as their liberation. Freeing people from their illusions does not stand in need of the same moral justification, if indeed it stands in need of any moral justification at all.

Think Different

Scott Adams has said about Steve Jobs that

> The biggest head-scratcher about Jobs's career is how many times he transformed entire industries: computers, phones, music, animation, and more. And each success happened with a different mix of Apple employees. Do you believe all of that success was luck, or perhaps luck plus extraordinary business skill? Or is it possible something else was happening? I don't believe in magic. But I can't rule out the possibility that reality has a user interface. Perhaps the Reality Distortion Field was exactly what it looked like. ("Reality Distortion Field")

Adams's point is that Jobs had a grasp on reality—or that he transformed reality. Either way, he did not have illusions, at least about the future. In her online article from 2000, Andrea Dudrow wrote:

> So what is it with Steve Jobs? Here's a notoriously cranky guy in charge of a relatively small computer company, from which he was once ousted in a boardroom coup, and who subsequently burned through most of $100 million trying (and failing) to start a successful business (remember Next Computer?)—and yet he is revered by fans and critics alike. ("Notes from the Epicenter")

But by the time of his death in 2011, Jobs, with the help of all of those he affected by his reality distortion field, had revolutionized not merely the personal computing industry (the Macintosh), but also the music industry (iTunes and the iPod), the phone industry (iPhone), digital books and magazines (the iPad), the digital content storage industry (iCloud), the animated film industry (Pixar), and the retail industry (the Apple Retail Store). Indeed, given that the World Wide Web was created on the NeXT Computer that Jobs designed after he was booted out of Apple in the mid-1980s, he may even take some credit for the existence of the web. By the time of his death in October 2011, the company that he founded, now simply known as Apple, Inc., was the most valuable company in the world, and he was the world's greatest CEO.

None of those people who did what they did under Jobs would have been able to do the things that they did without his having made them believe that the 'impossible' was, in fact, possible. His use of his reality distortion field was necessary, to get them to change their beliefs. To get them to *think different*. And thinking different was necessary for them to do what they did.

The result is that all of us now live in Steve Jobs's reality.

2
Counter-Culture Capitalist

CARRIE-ANN BIONDI

You guys were the rebels, man, the underdogs. But now, are you becoming The Man? Remember back in 1984, you had those awesome ads about overthrowing Big Brother? Look in the mirror, man!

—Jon Stewart on *The Daily Show*, April 20th, 2010

The name "Steve Jobs" has become synonymous with success. Apple products such as the wildly popular iPod and iPhone as well as the iMac computer have made him a household name in America. His self-made wealth and brash public persona might lead many to think that he is the epitome of the "greedy capitalist" looking only to maximize the bottom line.

Most people are surprised to learn that Jobs became successful precisely because he did not embody that stereotype. In fact, he possessed counter-cultural qualities and repeatedly placed himself at tremendous financial risk. In a touching move to set the record straight, his son, Reed, took aside one of Jobs's biographers to tell him that "his father was not a cold profit-seeking businessman but was motivated by a love of what he did and a pride in the products he was making" (*Steve Jobs*, p. 538). Jobs could have retired a multi-millionaire at age thirty, but he didn't. He strove to develop the best possible Apple products until he was too ill with cancer to do so.

Moreover, and perhaps even more surprising to many, Jobs is no exception in this regard. Contrary to popular belief, what drives capitalism, in the sense of genuinely free enterprise, is the creative individualism of idiosyncratic entrepreneurs. They are not afraid to stand outside the mainstream and pursue their own vision. These qualities allow them to "see gaps" of opportunity in the world. The alleged paradox of Jobs's counter-cultural attitude and capitalist success is only an apparent paradox.

The Alleged Paradox

In the popular imagination, the now infamous "one percent" at the top of the economic food chain is populated by conscienceless sharks like Gordon Gekko in *Wall Street* (1987) or callous managers like Bill Lumbergh in *Office Space* (1999). Alternatives to these images have been few. On the one hand, we have the virtuously struggling small business owner, such as George Bailey in *It's a Wonderful Life* (1946). On the other hand, we tolerate the successful business owner so long as he redeems his capitalist ways by engaging in philanthropy or has his income taxed heavily for redistributionist purposes. In philosophy, the classic version of tolerating economic success so long as it benefits "the least well off," is John Rawls's *A Theory of Justice*.

This makes nontraditional innovators like Jobs what Stephen Hicks calls "invisible" businesspeople. It's not that Jobs as a person was invisible. It would be nearly impossible for one of the world's youngest self-made billionaires not to have his image splashed all over the media. What has largely been absent from both popular and academic representations of the businessperson is the *kind* of businessperson Jobs embodies: the entrepreneur. Unlike the Gekko and Lumbergh types, entrepreneurs are not focused on maximizing profit or crushing others. Unlike the Bailey types, entrepreneurs do what they love in pursuit of their own vision and don't feel that they must be altruistic to justify what they do.

If it's true that businesspeople can best achieve capitalist success by seeking their bliss rather than the bottom line, then whence the stereotype of the greedy capitalist? An answer to this question is found partly in experience. We all know someone who resembles the tight-fisted, penny-pinching Ebenezer Scrooge from Charles Dickens's 1843 classic *A Christmas Carol*. But we can also look to the theory of human nature presented first in Plato's *Republic* and then in Thomas Hobbes's *Leviathan*. Their view of human nature influenced the nineteenth-century economic and political thought of Karl Marx and Friedrich Engels.

Plato, in his *Republic*, offers a famously long dialogue about the nature and value of justice. In it, Glaucon challenges Socrates to refute the popular view that people do (and should) act justly only because they are afraid of being punished if caught. Most people believe that *pleonexia* ("greed") is at the heart of human nature. That is, all people "desire to outdo others," and "what anyone's nature naturally pursues as good" is to "get more and more" without end. Although Socrates develops a lengthy response, this view of human nature as greedy and competitive has persisted. It resurfaces in Hobbes's seventeenth-century claim that "all mankind" has "a perpetual and restless desire of power after power, that ceaseth only in death." Plato and Hobbes would agree that capitalists, like all people, seek power and possessions, but that they are better than most at acquiring what they seek.

Marx and Engels share this view of human nature, and layer on a historical analysis of material and social conditions that lead to the emergence of capitalism. According to their theory, stages of history necessarily unfold with the growth of population. This creates pressure to increase production and develop new technology. The current stage of history is one of class antagonism, in which the bourgeoisie or capitalists (the few property owners) oppress the proletariat (the many propertyless workers). Oppression occurs because capitalists create private property laws to own the means of production so that they can protect what they can extort.

They then use their legally protected economic power to extract every ounce of productivity from propertyless workers through "wage slavery" in order to maximize profit. Workers become alienated from themselves, their products, and one another under such a system. No one sees his product as a craft that is part of himself, but rather as a thing that he makes only for the wage it brings. People then see themselves and others reduced to a "cash value," trading their alienated goods for others' alienated goods just to survive.

These thinkers' influence extends to the present day, largely shaping the public's assumption that business inherently treats people merely as expendable means in the endless pursuit of money. Such ideas are captured in Benjamin Barber's popular view about business, which in part targets Jobs: "McWorld . . . forges global markets rooted in consumption and profit" (*Jihad vs. McWorld*, pp. 6–7) and mesmerizes people everywhere with "fast music, fast computers, and fast food—MTV, Macintosh, and McDonald's" (p. 4). On Barber's view, globalized capitalism leads to homogenization and hedonism in its pursuit of the bottom line.

For those who rebel against capitalism (as it is depicted by writers like Marx, Engels, and Barber), the alternative is to fight "The Man." The Man is represented as a wealthy businessman in a suit and tie—a symbol of modernity's market-oriented status quo, with its alienation, large bureaucracy, and uniformity. Theodore Roszak dubs this the "technocracy," where a small group of "experts" efficiently manage as much of life as possible while excluding non-experts from the centers of power. The larger culture is controlled by being entertained with affordable consumer goods that distract them from what's going on. Counter-cultural renegades "drop out" of this production-and-consumption cycle and live outside the system, seeing business success as co-optation, selling out, and the death of individuality.

This adversarial juxtaposition of business and counter-culture has immense traction, as can be seen in Jon Stewart's half-joking challenge lobbed on *The Daily Show* at his friend Jobs. "You guys were the rebels, man, the underdogs.

But now, are you becoming The Man?" (*Steve Jobs*, p. 518). The incident concerned the 2010 controversy over which apps could be downloaded to the iPhone. Apple had decreed that pornography and controversial political cartoons could not be.

Given the socio-historical backdrop, we can see why "counter-cultural capitalism" is generally regarded as a contradiction.

Ways of Being Counter-Cultural

To understand why counter-culture and capitalism are not inherently enemies, we first need to unpack the idea of "counter-culture." The obvious and basic sense of the phrase is for us to be in opposition to our culture. What it means to be counter-cultural thus depends on the content of the culture that we're opposed to, which is also relative to a time period. Since cultures are not monolithic, we also need to specify the features of the culture that we refuse to accept.

Just as important as the content of a culture that one is countering is the *way* in which individuals can go against the norms of the larger culture. There are at least three different ways in which people can be counter-cultural: existential, emotional, and cognitive (thanks to David Kelley for suggesting this terminology). These three counter-cultural categories are often associated with specific time periods or societies. However, since these are ways of being that are independent of content, they can be manifested by anyone who counters any culture at any time.

Existential counter-culture is marked by rejection of the world as such and whatever rules and norms exist in that world. Since adults are those who create the rules and laws, the saying "Don't trust anyone over thirty" became popular with the existential counter-culture crowd. Experimentation is exalted as a way to alter one's perception of reality, to "drop out" of it for a while. This kind of counter-culture was popularized by the hippie movement of the 1960s and 1970s. They embraced Timothy Leary's advocacy of psychedelic drugs, the folk and rock music of artists such as Bob Dylan and Janis Joplin, and the Beat poetry of Allen Ginsberg.

Those who are emotionally counter-cultural endorse the Romantic notion of passionate self-expression. Romanticism's heyday occurred during the late eighteenth through mid-nineteenth century with literary figures such as William Wordsworth and Johann Goethe. Romantics rebel against the Enlightenment value of reason as well as the scientific method and the Industrial Revolution. They tend to exalt nature over civilization, and idealize the Bohemian image of the starving artist in a garret who must suffer for "living his truth."

Cognitive counter-culture exists when we reflectively choose our own values distinct from (and often counter to) what others believe. A few traits are distinctive of this kind of counter-culture. These include independence of mind, using reason to reach autonomously held beliefs, integrity, and the courage to take risks and stand alone in our convictions. Unlike the first two kinds of counter-culture, this one is explicitly more intellectual and is not suspicious of technology or science.

A prominent example of this less-discussed form of counter-culture is "techno-geek," which overlapped with and outlived hippie counter-culture. Techno-geeks devoured the crypto-libertarian science fiction of authors like Robert Heinlein, and they ushered in the computer revolution. They started out tinkering with circuit boards in garages and hacking into computer and phone systems, and later became computer engineering and programming titans in Silicon Valley. As we learn from Luke Dormehl's *Apple Revolution*, these individuals comprised the large bulk of Jobs's milieu, sharing with him the desire "to claim high-tech for the masses" (p. 7). They wanted to create personal computers as "a tool of liberation" (p. 21), so that people could live authentically as informed individuals.

The Entrepreneurial Spirit Solution

Within capitalism, some people may be driven toward business pursuits by purely monetary goals. They might sometimes even be financially successful in doing so. However, that is not what resides at the heart of satisfying and meaningful long-term business success.

Entrepreneurs manifest a variety of traits, including creativity, courage, initiative, perseverance, integrity, and resilience in the face of failure. Such individuals typically work long hours and many years without vacations, intent on solving puzzles and engaging with tasks they love that push them to the limits of their intellect and endurance (see the article by Stephen Hicks and the contributions to *Be the Solution*). These are characteristics that they share in common with those who are cognitively counter-cultural. The asset of greatest (personal and social) value is what Ayn Rand calls "the creative mind." We need to develop our minds at least to some degree through conscious choice in order to be productive in the task of living. Creativity is the bedrock on which we can build more actualized forms of productivity through entrepreneurship. Breakthroughs are possible when we give our mind free rein to think beyond the constraints of what has been created before.

The creativity of those engaging in pursuits that liberate our potential for bringing value into the world is but a necessary precondition for offering something that others wish to trade for. Mihaly Csikszentmihalyi underscores the point that successful entrepreneurship requires more than the personal creativity that often accompanies counter-cultural personalities. It also requires the right context and social conditions for the creative individual to succeed. Creativity exists when someone introduces a new idea or product into some specific domain (such as computers) and those who are somehow responsible for that domain allow the change to take hold.

Csikszentmihalyi observes that creativity is fostered best in societies that protect wealth-creation and allow space for innovation to exist and be recognized. Rand recognizes this in her moral defense of capitalism, arguing that it is a system that empowers individuals with the freedom to create and be rewarded for their efforts ("What Is Capitalism?").

Steve Jobs also sees the link between free markets and innovation: "If people copied or stole our software, we'd be out of business. If it weren't protected, there'd be no incentive for us to make new software or product designs. If protection of intellectual property begins to disappear, creative companies will disappear or never get started" (*Apple Revolution*, pp. 430–31).

The iCon

Steve Jobs became a multi-media business giant precisely because his counter-cultural attitude and charismatic personality came along in the socially liberating decades of late-twentieth-century America. Dreams could come true from good ideas and scraps of metal welded on a workbench in teenagers' garages.

As a youth, it was clear that Jobs was outside the mainstream. He was anti-authoritarian and fiercely individualistic, feeling free to ignore rules that didn't make sense to him, experiment with drugs, and drop out of Reed College. He was a fruitarian, fasted, and was devoted in his own way to Zen Buddhism (*iCon*, pp. 12–22). This is where his similarities to existential and emotional counter-culturalism end, however.

Jobs was no stereotypical non-conformist. He enthusiastically took his share of psychedelic drugs, but did not embrace "the hippie ethic of putting out the least possible effort" (p. 17). Beneath his hippie exterior was a passionate drive to create and to succeed. As he put it, he wanted to "put a ding in the universe" (*Apple Revolution*, p. 43). Jobs's objective was not to counter capitalism, but to change the world. In order to do this, he drew on the best talent from the cognitive counter-cultural milieu he grew up in. Launching a series of brilliant advertising campaigns, he pitted Apple "underdog" techno-geeks against "Establishment" computer giants such as Bill Gates and IBM who represented conventional mediocrity and impersonality.

Seeing that Jobs was exceptionally driven to succeed at what he was passionate about, key figures in his life looked past his hippie exterior and recognized something special, something they had no idea at the time would change the world. According to Al Alcorn, Atari's chief engineer who hired Jobs in 1974, Jobs came to the interview "dressed in rags basically, hippie stuff. . . . he was determined to have the job and there was some spark. I really saw the spark in that man, some inner energy, an attitude that he was going to get it done. And he had a vision, too" (p. 23). That vision, combined with the prescience to surround himself with uniquely talented and driven individuals like Steve Wozniak and John Lasseter, led Jobs to found Apple Computer and invest in Pixar. He guided them through financially and personally rocky times to triumph when their innovative products connected with consumers.

Any brief analysis of the positive traits that made Jobs a successful businessperson is bound to oversimplify and push aside other qualities. Being counter-cultural has an abrasive side unconcerned with what others think or with observing conventions that grease the wheels of social interaction. His charismatic personality was a double-edged sword that helped him to create possibilities but also alienate people. He was impatient, quick to judge, and sharp-tongued in ways that left hurt feelings in his wake. He was a demanding perfectionist who expected others to work as hard and care as much about his work as he did. Jobs succeeded when he pulled in the right people and offered a product that found his market's pulse. He didn't succeed when his sometimes childish temper and insistence that his idea was valuable even when there was not a large enough market to sustain it prevailed.

The benefits of Jobs's brash personality far outweighed its disadvantages, however, particularly when tempered by time, experience, and parenthood. His strong inclination to march to the beat of his own drum as well as his knack for imagining himself into the role of a potential product user allowed him to unleash new ideas that the public discovered it wanted. Even *Newsweek*'s Daniel Lyons, who had snarkily railed in print against the iPad, changed his tune. Lyons admits that Jobs "has an uncanny ability to cook up gadgets that we didn't know we needed, but then suddenly we can't live without" (*Steve Jobs*, p. 496).

One could quote any number of things that Jobs said that reflect his counter-cultural attitude and creative entrepreneurship. For example, in a presentation about the iPad, he emphasized that it embodied "one of the themes of his life," saying, "The reason Apple can create products like the iPad is that we've always tried to be at the intersection of technology and the liberal arts" (p. 494). That intersection is where the next "gap" for innovation will exist, and Jobs wanted to be there to embrace it. When reflecting on his legacy, Jobs explains his drive to innovate:

> You always have to keep pushing to innovate. . . . Dylan could have sung protest songs forever and probably made a lot of money, but he didn't. He had to move on, and when he did, by going electric in 1965, he alienated a lot of people. . . . The Beatles were the same way. They kept evolving, moving, refining their art. That's what I've always tried to do—keep moving. Otherwise, as Dylan says, if you're not busy being born, you're busy dying. . . . What drove me? . . . It's about trying to express something in the only way that most of us know how—because we can't write Bob Dylan songs or Tom Stoppard plays. We try to use the talents we do have to express our deep feelings, to show appreciation of all the contributions that came before us, and to add something to that flow. That's what has driven me. (Isaacson, *Steve Jobs*, p. 570)

These are the words of someone who embraces the multifaceted ways of being human without reducing our complexity. Indeed, he celebrates it. From Apple's iconic logo that symbolizes taking a bite of knowledge to the "think different" advertising campaign, Jobs was all about empowering the individual. He summarizes Apple's vision at the 1997 Macworld Expo:

> I think you still have to think differently to buy an Apple computer. . . . they are the creative spirits in this world. They are the people

that are not just out to get a job done; they are out to change the world. . . . And we make tools for those kinds of people. (Dormehl, *Apple Revolution*, pp. 394–95)

Ultimately, though, it is what Jobs produced—both his character and tangible goods—that provides a testament to the inextricable connection between counter-culture and capitalism. The life and work of Steve Jobs reflect the truth in Robert Frost's insightful lines: "Two roads diverged in a wood, and I—I took the one less traveled by, and that has made all the difference."

And what a difference Steve Jobs has made. The next time you download a song from iTunes, remember that this was made possible in no small measure by a person who jeopardized his first Silicon Valley job with Atari so as to journey to "see his guru" in India and got demoted from chairman of the board of and then resigned from Apple Computer—his own company—when his idiosyncratic ways clashed too much with others (*iCon*, pp. 23, 31, 115–129). Jobs was a person who could think outside the box so well that he could put a world of music and access to information in the palm of your hand.[1]

---

[1] I am grateful to Kurt Keefner, Shawn Klein, and Joshua Zader, as well as all of the members of The Atlas Society's monthly online seminar group, for their generous and valuable feedback on an earlier version of this essay, and to David Kelley for proposing the terminology of existential, emotional, and cognitive ways of being counter-cultural.

3
The Anti-Social Creator

Terry W. Noel

Steve Jobs was an obnoxious, condescending, and vindictive man who berated and belittled his employees. He was also one of the greatest technological visionaries of all time. Jobs radically transformed the personal computer industry, the music industry, the movie industry, and the telecommunications industry. Chances are that the reader of this book has used at least one Apple device or watched a movie made by Pixar. Jobs's efforts resulted in the technological betterment of millions.

But was he a virtuous man?

The Four Cardinal Virtues

Philosophers have been talking about virtues for thousands of years, and in all their discussions they keep coming back to a short list of character traits, known as the four cardinal virtues:

- **Prudence**
- **Justice**
- **Courage**
- **Temperance**

Judging by these four classic virtues, Jobs was hardly a virtuous man. While at times he displayed traits from this list, his rabid need to achieve led him to violate them regularly. Yet his products changed the world forever—for the good. Isn't this what we mean by being virtuous—doing good things?

So here's the puzzle. How can a man do so much good while being deficient in the classic virtues? And does this mean we have to rethink these virtues and come up with a different list?

Jobs and the Four Cardinal Virtues

Prudence

Many people have considered *prudence* foremost among the virtues. Though today we think of prudence more in terms of caution, the original sense of the word was the ability to make right decisions. However, according to Alan Deutschman's account, Jobs was notorious for making *bad* decisions. After being thrown out of Apple (in part due to a bad decision about the Lisa, a computer that flopped) he built a new computer company (NeXT) whose products had no clear market, were too expensive, and sold abysmally few units.

On the other hand, Jobs shows us some compelling reasons *not* to be prudent. Despite his numerous mistakes, he emerged a hero as he came back to Apple and took Apple from near-bankruptcy to its ranking as the most valuable company in the world. Mistakes are the bread and butter of the entrepreneurial process, without which no progress can be made. For entrepreneurs, prudence can mean death by timidity.

Even if prudence were accepted as a desirable character trait, it is not clear it would do an entrepreneur any good. One reason is the sheer uncertainty of entrepreneurial markets. The prudent person needs something to go on, some evidence that a decision will lead to the desired outcome. For new products, especially radical innovations, there simply is no history of similar decisions. One cannot "strike a balance" between two extremes because those extremes are not well-defined.

Justice

Justice is the balance between self-aggrandizement and self-sacrifice—assuring that each receives what they are due. Jobs was routinely in violation of this virtue. He was maniacal about secrecy at Apple. He shut down bloggers, even those favorable to his products, by threatening lawsuits to force them to reveal their sources. (See Bryan Gardiner's account.) Jobs always had to be the center of attention, the person who was seen as the smartest guy in the room. He had to be the one on the stage for a new product release and the one to whom accolades flowed. He was a *prima donna*.

You may be forgiven for taking risks and failing, but to claim credit or allocate rewards unfairly seems both wrong and deeply offensive. Aside from its intuitive appeal, justice has a practical advantage. Being just endears you to others and sets up social relations that make future interactions go more smoothly. In the case of someone setting out to change the world, however, such niceties may get in the way.

One example is Jobs's appropriation of the Graphical User Interface (GUI). Even after they became practical for military and industrial use, computers remained highly specialized equipment that could only be operated after extensive training. The computer-human interface was lightly considered, there being no particular reason to make them broadly human-friendly. Only a few people would ever even see a computer, much less have occasion to use it. That is, until Apple.

Our present ability to interact with computers in an intuitive and user-friendly way are due largely to Steve Jobs. However, he was not the originator of the ideas that enabled it. As Walter Isaacson tells it, Jobs's vision of a "friendly" computer was inspired at least in part by a visit to Xerox's Palo Alto Research Center in 1979. He saw a remarkable thing—the icons-and-mouse system that is near-universal today. By 1984 he had improved upon what he saw and built the Apple Macintosh, changing the personal computer market forever.

Jobs had not created GUI; he had essentially stolen it. Though later court cases would establish that Apple had not legally infringed on Xerox's patents, it was clear that Jobs had taken liberally from the idea he had seen at PARC. Eventually, even he admitted as much, saying, "It's more fun to be a pirate than to join the navy."

Jobs could easily have been humble. He could have credited Xerox. He could have paid no mind to bloggers whose speculation on new products stole his thunder. He could have directed attention away from himself and acted the part of the humble servant-leader. Doing so might have made him appear to be more just, but also would have diminished the leverage he had with the marketplace. Truly new ideas are rare. For people to embrace them immediately is even rarer. Radical ideas require radical marketing and precise market positioning. Humble, self-effacing people don't have the audacity to make this kind of thing happen. Jobs did—and his being in the spotlight was part of what made it happen.

Temperance

Temperance was not one of Jobs's strong suits either. He was not given to restraint in his personal life, constantly going on bizarre diets and following short-term obsessions with a vengeance. As a virtue, temperance keeps us in check lest our passions be our undoing, at least when our passions are about to lead us to do something dumb. Jobs was not governed by temperance in any significant way.

However, passion also has the capacity to transform a human being into a creative powerhouse. Jobs described himself once as a "hopeless romantic" who "wanted to make a difference." (See the article in *Entrepreneur*.) In his case, this passion often turned him into a cruel, condescending heel. Deutschman reports that Jobs once looked at an employee's work and said, "You've baked a lovely cake and used dogshit for icing." Such outbursts were routine at Apple, making you wonder how he kept employees at all. But the end result over the years was a core of deeply committed people who could withstand his barrages and use them to fuel even greater efforts toward perfection.

Courage

Last, *courage*. Of the four classic virtues, Steve Jobs probably exemplified this one the most. His willingness to try new things even after abject failures is inspiring. In the case of Pixar, Jobs's fortitude paid off as the company released the wildly successful movie *Toy Story*. NeXT paid off as well when it was sold to Apple and its software used to develop the OSX operating system.

Yet this kind of behavior is a different type of courage. For entrepreneurs to be successful, they must be brash. Not courageous, brash. Mere courage dictates that an individual act so as to stand up for the good, but not do so foolishly. Being an entrepreneur often requires a kind of foolish confidence that you'll win no matter what the odds.

This is not to say that fools invariably win. Jobs had another type of courage that enabled him to turn a flaming failure into a glowing success—the ability to change his mind: Apple CEO Tim Cook noted that Jobs:

> had the ability to change his mind, much more so than anyone I've ever met. . . . Maybe the most underappreciated thing about Steve was that he had the courage to change his mind. (Quoted in *Steve Jobs*)

So while it can be argued that Jobs had courage, his particular brand of it was a unique twist on an old virtue.

The Virtues of an Entrepreneur

In the light of the four cardinal virtues, then, Jobs was not so virtuous. Part of the reason may be that the creator, the visionary, and the entrepreneur do not fit neatly into this plain vanilla view of virtue. In some ways, they are a breed apart. Jobs never considered himself to be bound by the rules others followed.

Though this trait was no doubt irritating and obnoxious, it is probably good for the rest of us that Jobs did not consider himself a member of the pack. While some might consider such an attitude narcissistic and a reflection of poor character, it also enabled him to do what few could—radically transform the world for the better. Jobs was simply too big in his own mind to be bound by petty social mores—and it worked.

Entrepreneurs by definition change reality. They create new worlds, sometimes drastically altering our perceptions of what is possible. In order to shake others out of their complacency, they sometimes resort to unorthodox methods. Jobs was devastatingly effective at using a combination of charm and condescension, delivered with surgical precision. An employee once coined the phrase "reality distortion field" to describe the effect Jobs had on his listeners:

> If you trust him, you can do things. . . . If he's decided to make something happen, then he's just going to make it happen. (Quoted in *Steve Jobs*)

Everything about Steve Jobs raises questions about what we mean by virtue in visionary leaders. When we say that a person on the street is virtuous, we're often speaking of a kind of blasé goodness. We expect someone who does the "right" thing. We do not envision this individual to be a maverick or a person of exceptional creative accomplishment. The four cardinal virtues leave little room for the exceptional individual.

Does that mean we need to add to our common conception of virtue to include those traits that successful entrepreneurs possess? It seems odd to assert that the entrepreneur should have a *different* set of virtues than the rest of us. It smacks of a "means justifying the ends" mentality. It is also reminiscent of Nietzsche's master-slave morality—one set of rules for the lions, another for the lambs.

On the other hand, Nietzsche also states in *The Will to Power* that "the highest man is he who determines values and directs the will of millennia by giving direction to the highest natures." Was Jobs one of these men? Did he direct the will of others by showing them what they wanted instead of asking them? I suggest that he was. "You can't just ask customers what they want," Isaacson reports him as saying, quoting Henry Ford, who first organized the mass production of the family car: "If I had asked them what they wanted, they would have said a faster horse."

Entrepreneurs are not ordinary. They disrupt routines. They shake up people's sensibilities. They kill off old ideas and introduce new ones. They are the wellspring from which progress flows. The four cardinal virtues are a good guide for the ordinary citizen choosing to fit in and be good. For the entrepreneur, they are deadly. In their stead, I suggest that the following three traits are foundational to the virtuous entrepreneur: independence of mind, vision, and audacity.

Independence of Mind

The virtuous entrepreneur is a person of intellectual integrity. They rely on the judgment of their own mind over the thoughts and feelings of others. Concerned less with fitting in than with standing out, the entrepreneur values individuality above all.

Vision

The ability to see what the future can be is vision. Successful entrepreneurs are able not only to convey the limits of the status quo, but to communicate a vivid image of what the future can be. Truly great entrepreneurs see things that most people cannot fathom until they see the new product or idea in action.

Audacity

Audacious people are not only bold, they are often impudent. Steve Jobs make no secret of the fact that he thought of himself as the smartest guy in the room. For entrepreneurs, modesty and restraint are not always helpful in achieving their goals. Entrepreneurs must press forward with a boldness that defies common social norms.

Not Fitting In

The ancient Egyptians recognized that certain broad characteristics of the universe were better for humans than others. Their goddess Maat was the Egyptian personification of these characteristics—balance, order, and justice. Isfet, her counterpart, symbolized chaos and injustice. One led to good for humanity; the other to destruction and deprivation.

As Maria Isabel Pita explains, Maat served the Egyptians as the spirit of justice that informed individual behavior in the context of society. Virtue was living in accordance with Maat, and failing to live in accordance with Maat was thought to bring punishment on King and commoner alike.

The ancient Greeks further refined the concept of virtue. In the *Republic,* Plato wrote of the same four traits that today we call cardinal virtues. A bit later, Aristotle's contribution in his *Nicomachean Ethics* was to define virtue as a mean between two extremes, sometimes called the Golden Mean.

The fact that virtue was defined as a "mean" for Aristotle, however, didn't make it a formulaic rule. He emphasized that particular decisions about where the mean lies hinge on the situation, your expertise, and your level of moral development. However, Aristotle did establish balance and moderation as key components of virtue. This sense of virtue as moderation informs religious and philosophical traditions all over the world. Confucianism, Buddhism, Stoicism, and Christianity all contain some version of these four building blocks of character. How does Steve Jobs stack up against them?

Since the first codification of virtue by the Ancient Egyptians, virtue has been conceived of as both a personal and a societal affair. You should be good, but you should also "fit in" for the benefit of the society. Virtuous people, by the standards of the four cardinal virtues, may have influence in a community, but will rarely be disruptive.

The problem with such a state of affairs is precisely that it *is* staid and predictable. Were it not for the disruption caused by creative thinkers, we would still be lighting oil lamps by which to peruse scrolls. Instead we have iPads and iPods to light up our lives with knowledge and music. These things come to exist precisely because people like Steve Jobs don't think the four cardinal virtues apply to them.

Being virtuous in the sense of cultivating the four cardinal virtues no doubt benefits the individual possessing them, but not in every sense. If your goal is to lead a quiet life, contribute to mankind positively but unobtrusively, and be thought of well by others, this is the ticket. Fitting in, however, only benefits those individuals whose inclinations run toward conformity. For rebels like Jobs, the four virtues are prison walls.

In myths and legends we can find the theme of the anti-social creator, the individual who contributes something just because he won't fit in. Described by Joseph Campbell in *The Hero with a Thousand Faces,* the path a true benefactor of mankind takes is one of rejecting society's norms and going out on their own. In the language of mythology, the hero (in our case, the entrepreneur) gets the "call" and sets off to places others dare not go. Along the way, he finds both great opportunity and great danger. Success or even survival are far from certain.

Failure to answer the call results in a life lived falsely. We all know someone who has sacrificed their dreams to the unfulfilling comfort of a cubicle. For true creators, inventors, artists, and entrepreneurs, this is not an option, nor would they find solace in knowing that they had been prudent, just, temperate, and brave rather than independent, audacious visionaries.

Jobs was not cubicle-farm material, and while his entrepreneurial virtues cost him dearly in personal relationships and physical health, they also made him more than he could have been otherwise. He set out to change the world and did. Few people can look in the mirror and say that honestly.

While this answers the question of how the three entrepreneurial virtues benefit the individual, what is their relation to society? The renegade's personal virtues bring value to society, but in a paradoxical way. Upon his or her return from the journey precipitated by the call, the hero brings a boon back to society, but sometimes the people do not want it or can't understand it at first.

Moses brought down the Ten Commandments to a people that had forsaken Yahweh. In the end, Buddha despaired of transmitting his teaching to others and upon his deathbed admonished his followers to "Be a lamp unto yourself." Jobs's thinking about the role of technology in the lives of everyday people was so far ahead of the norm that he often launched market failures. Society may crave compliance, but it benefits from audacity.

Just as the hero of myth turns the notion of social propriety on its head, so does the entrepreneur require a different set of virtues to guide him. The person living by these virtues has a flourishing life, as Aristotle would say, but it is probably more colorful than Aristotle had in mind. They are virtues, nonetheless. The result is not only an assent to life for the individual, but a gift to the society in which he lives.

4
What Pixar Taught Millennials about Personhood

KYLE MUNKITTRICK

Yep, we're going to be talking about kids' movies and one of the most contentious concepts in bioethics. Take a moment and think about your favorite scene from your favorite Pixar movie. Remember how it made you feel, why you love it, and just what the characters were doing. Got it? Great.

With our mental stages set, let's begin our foray into understanding how Pixar just might have inadvertently primed a generation to accept non-humans as persons.

I *love* Pixar. From the elegant animation, to the finely-wrought characters, to the truly original stories, to the emotional depth of the narrative, there is little to *not* love about their films. Given the caliber of those involved with Pixar throughout its life (LucasFilm, Steve Jobs, John Lassiter, Brad Bird, Andrew Stanton, and Disney, to name a few), the almost impossibly consistent quality of Pixar Animation Studios becomes a bit more believable. Pixar films are, in the fullest definition of the words, both wonderful and awesome.

Steve Jobs was the true parent of Pixar. While the seeds of Pixar were started at LucasFilm, it was not until Jobs spun the company off into an independent studio in 1986 that Pixar was truly born (see Pixar's "Our Story").

However, in the unfortunate circumstance that you are not a Pixar fanatic, you still have a stake in this discussion. The much maligned Millennial Generation (of which I am one proud member) is on the precipice of becoming a hugely influential part of society. Over the coming years, Millennials will be voting, buying, and teaching. And for all our flaws, Millennials have one huge advantage—we were raised on Pixar.

Disregard the critical acclaim, ignore the millions of parents and grandparents who watched these movies with their kids. Instead, just consider that the next generation of leaders and decision makers has been exposed to the concepts I'm about to outline as an essential and enormous part of their formative years. Whether or not you like Pixar (which how could you not, you monster?), their influence on us is going to affect you for years to come.

What, you may well be asking by this point, is the idea that Pixar has planted in so many of our minds? How do stories about the fishes in our fish tanks and the bugs in our backyard stand poised to influence the future of rights and morality?

My thesis is simple: Pixar movies teach us how to recognize and accept personhood wherever we may find it, particularly among non-humans.

Recognizing Personhood

Before we can dive into how Pixar teaches us to recognize personhood, we've got to make sure we're all on the same page as to what personhood is. That's going to be a bit tough because, you see, "personhood" as a concept has a problem: no one seems to be able to define it. Though not due to a shortage of submissions, I grant you that.

The basic premise of personhood seems obvious enough: we grant rights and moral standing not based on someone merely being human, but based on their cognitive ability and the way they behave. This collection of abilities and behaviors is known holistically as "personhood."

Personhood is why we wait until you're eighteen to let you vote or twenty-one to let you drink or thirty-five to let you run for President (in the States at least). The law makes sense until you frame it as, "Why are some human beings allowed to vote and others are not?" The answer is "Because a newborn human being does not have the same moral agency and responsibility as its thirty-something human parent." Human history is a continuous effort to figure out *who* has the traits that constitute personhood and who doesn't.

So far most modern countries have figured out a lot of stuff that *doesn't* affect personhood (owning property, race, gender, religion, to name a few). Age still seems to be a pretty good indicator of personhood, but we're working on ruling out a few other things (such as species, or organic composition). Any fight for civil rights is a fight for personhood. It conveys citizenship, rights, autonomy, and moral agency. But wait a second, didn't I *just say* that no one is able to define what personhood even *is*? How in the world are we basing fundamental aspects of rights around something no one is really able to define?

The problem here is not lack of definitions or explanations of personhood, but of agreement. Many definitions seem to come *very* close to articulating a comprehensive and reliable spectrum of personhood.[1] Everything from a pebble to a parrot to a politician can be placed on these better spectrums. These spectrums of personhood list a series of traits and behaviors: for example a trait might be that "A person can recognize other persons." There is a sticking point here—one can ask, "What does it mean for something to 'recognize other persons'?" Moreover, is it even *possible* to recognize other persons?

For philosophers, the "Problem of Other Minds" is the problem that arises from not being able to prove that anyone else is conscious. We know that we're conscious because we experience it directly, but can we prove that others have experiences too? We can only see what they look like and what they do; we can't directly see what they're thinking or feeling. We've got evidence for it from their behavior, but we can't prove it without a doubt. This conundrum is a big deal for personhood, because if we can't prove that other humans

---

[1] I personally am a fan of the criteria of personhood given by Herzing and White in "Dolphins and the Question of Personhood."

have consciousness, when we're quite certain that they do, how do we begin to prove consciousness in things alien to us, like animals, machines, or literal aliens?

There's a lot to debate, and that's only *one item* on *one list* of criteria to be a person. So it is we come to the first general problem of personhood (no matter how you define it): we don't really agree on what the various "traits" of personhood usually mean.

Round in Circles

The next problem with personhood is that we are usually stuck with listing traits that are inevitably circular. Take the oft-cited personhood criterion of "long-term planning." Long-term planning is simply being able to sacrifice a short-term desire for long-term gains. For example, a squirrel storing nuts for the winter is only doing short-term planning. Long-term planning would be that same squirrel leaving a few acorns planted so that his or her offspring had a richer bounty in years to come (or, say, taking out a loan to buy an orchard). We don't see *intentional* long-term planning (forgetting where you buried all your acorns doesn't count) in squirrels, so they probably aren't full persons.

However, the behavior of future planning is absent in a good number of those we consider full persons and, yet, we do not deny their personhood. In fact, we often find the inability to live up to a given standard of personhood to be a moral failing among those we perceive as persons. Nearly all aspects of personhood have one of two effects, they support the claim that a person is either a moral patient (worthy of ethical treatment) or a moral agent (responsible to treat others ethically). We perceive failings in those who have the *capacity* for ethical behaviors (and therefore responsibility for ethical behaviors) and do not exhibit them. We assume this capacity based on the observations of other behaviors that imply personhood.

So, the logical question follows: how do you know if someone (or something) has the *capacity* for some behavior? Why do we judge a person who doesn't plan ahead but not the aforementioned squirrel? Well, we can't just crack the skull open and look at your brain. There is no "tool use" section of the brain, nor a "long-term planning" part of the brain.

That's not to say we have no idea what parts of the brain do. We've actually got a pretty decent map. For example, the prefrontal cortex is generally associated with things like moral reasoning, empathy, and future planning. Other personhood traits like language, have many subareas that are extremely well defined, such as "Broca's area" of the brain. Yet even these are simply spots we've identified that affect how the mind works when damaged. If something doesn't have a prefrontal cortex, we can probably bet it doesn't have personhood. The problem is that lots of things have a prefrontal cortex and we aren't sure what exactly in that part of the brain is necessary to make personhood a certainty. We don't fundamentally understand the underlying structure that differentiates these areas from others, nor do we have complete modeling of any given trait. So, examining the brain alone isn't enough for us to determine if there is a mind.

We may suppose that we really only have one way of assessing whether something is a person with a mind: watching what it does. But can behavior really tell us everything? John Searle's Chinese Room experiment does a darn good job of making you doubt that you can judge internal workings by observing external behaviors. In Searle's thought experiment, you're in a room with a comprehensive rulebook for responding to Chinese symbols. A symbol comes to you through slot A, you follow your rulebook, write the appropriate symbol on a piece of paper, and push it thru slot B. You don't understand Chinese, but to those outside the room it appears as though you do (or, perhaps, the room itself does). Extend the analogy to something like a computer and the point is clear: just because something responds *as if* it understands does not mean it truly does.

Okay, so we've got something of a knot here. Personhood can't be defined very well because the traits that comprise it are contentious, ill-defined themselves, or the definitions are circular. Personhood can't be properly identified because behaviors don't actually provide evidence for the way internal processes work. Well, crap.

To get out of this philosophical corner we've backed ourselves into let's look at how we treat our fellow human beings in reality. None of us walks around with a personhood checklist, yet we do a pretty good job of identifying persons in our day-to-day life. Despite having all the right parts of the brain, babies lack nearly every qualifier of personhood save for being alive and able to respond to stimulus. We somehow know this *intuitively* through interaction and observation. Even when we don't understand how the Chinese Room of our minds works, we get along just fine. We base judgments of personhood on the actions we observe, because that's all we've got, folks.

So what do we know about identifying personhood? First, that lists of personhood traits are all ultimately dependent on observations of behavior. Second, and perhaps more important, that even without a comprehensive definition of personhood (or even anything resembling a consensus of what personhood is) we seem to *intuitively be able to identify those who possess it and to what degree they possess it* by comparing others to ourselves. History backs this up. Anytime any group has gained rights, it hasn't been by arguing they tick all the boxes of personhood, it's been based on ineffable, intuitive evidence that "they" (those without rights) are the same as "we" (those with rights).

My argument is *not* that personhood can't be defined. It's that intuitive identification of personhood has proved sufficient thus far to grant rights (I suspect it will do us good for a while still). And it is with this intuitive sensing of personhood that we return to Pixar.

In Toon with the Non-Human

To understand how Pixar movies have primed us for non-human personhood, we've got to go back to the year before

Toy Story was released—to be precise, 1994 and Disney's *The Lion King*. On top of being my favorite Shakespeare adaptation, *The Lion King* is the only Disney movie to date with zero references to the existence of human beings. This is important because how Pixar deals with humans informs how they deal with *non-humans*.

Disney and Pixar rarely have humans as the sole intelligent entities in their movies. Excluding plots requiring magic, non-human characters in Disney films are either anthropomorphous animals (walking upright, wearing clothes, shooting bows and arrows) that take the place of human characters (such as *Robin Hood*) or are animals with a preternatural awareness of and ability to interact with feral human beings (for instance *The Jungle Book* or *Tarzan*). *The Lion King* stands out in that the universe is purely animal. There is no trash on the Serengeti, no airplanes flying over, no animals wearing hats or walking unnaturally on their hind legs. You can't even date when the story takes place, because there are no human references from which to calculate an approximation. Save for the fact that Zazu knows "I've Got a Lovely Bunch of Coconuts," there is no evidence that the characters within *The Lion King* even know humans exist.

The Lion King gives us a clean slate. We know what a non-human world looks like. Now we can tackle how Pixar handles people, which, in turn, will tell us more about how Pixar handles personhood. (I'm not going to include *Cars*, *Cars 2*, and *Brave* in my discussion, because the *Cars* universe is too extreme an alternate reality and *Brave* relies on magic.)

The relationship between humans and the non-human characters is particular to Pixar films. There are certain general patterns that make things far more interesting than the average Disney fairy tale. First, there's no magic. No problems are caused or fixed by the wave of a wand. Second, Pixar films happen in the world of human beings. Even in films like a *A Bug's Life* and *Finding Nemo*, in which humans only exist as backdrops for the action, humanity's presence in the story is felt. These first two patterns are simple: Pixar characters inhabit a universe that is non-magical and co-inhabited by humans.

Human as Partner to Non-Human

The third pattern, built on top of the first two, is that at least one main character is an intelligent being that is not a human. There are two types of human roles in Pixar movies. The first is Human as Antagonist. In movies like *Toy Story* (1, 2, and 3), *A Bug's Life*, and *Finding Nemo*, the protagonists are all non-human. Ancillary characters like Sid, the Collector, and Darla could be more accurately described as environmental antagonists than proper characters.

The second type of human role is Human as Partner. In these films, the main character befriends a human being as part of the hero's journey: Remy, Colette, and Linguini; WALL-E, EVE, Mary, and John; Sully, Mike, and Boo; Russell, Carl, Kevin, and Dug. These are the heroic teams of their respective movies.

You can see where I'm going here. Particularly in *Monsters Inc*, *WALL-E*, *Ratatouille*, and *Up!* there's no ambiguity about the reality of intelligence in the non-human characters. In each of these we are asked to accept one deviation from our reality. While it seems different in every case (monsters are real, robots can fall in love, fish have a sense of family, dogs can talk, a rat can cook), the simple fact is that Pixar only asks us to accept one idea over and over and over again: Non-humans can be sentient, sapient, intelligent, moral beings. That's the central difference between Pixar's universe and our current reality.

What makes this idea so astonishing and the message so powerful is that the story arc of the Human as Partner narrative is a *positive* one. In each case, the story begins with a non-human living among a familiar setting. Be it WALL-E alone among the garbage, Remy with his massive extended rodent family, or Sully and Mike Wazowski on their way to work, we're introduced to the hero in relative normalcy. We are endeared to these characters because they are special:

Remy wants to cook. WALL-E is in love. In each case, our heroes make the decision to go outside of the rules of their society to pursue a higher goal. In each case, they are ostracized for their aberrant behavior.

In being ostracized, however, the non-human encounters a human. Remy, lost in the kitchen, meets Linguini. WALL-E literally bumps into both John and Mary. The deviation from normal behavior acts as a catalyst for the first interaction.

Now we come to the second essential piece of the Human as Partner narrative: the human as deviant. Boo is not afraid of monsters. John and Mary (the two people who help WALL-E and EVE) get out of their hover chairs and look away from the screens. Carl escapes the old folks' home with a balloon-house airship. A team is formed when the mutual outsiders recognize a shared sense of purpose. Human and non-human rebels alike seek out one another. In combining efforts, however, the team doubles their opposition, with the non-human and human normative majorities rejecting and condemning their behavior. In *Ratatouille*, Remy is criticized by his father and alienates his friends while Linguini loses the respect of the entire kitchen and is at risk of having the restaurant closed for health violations. There is a high cost for non-conformity.

The new is seen as dangerous and therefore feared. Pixar movies with the Human as Partner narrative emphasize that should a non-human intelligence arise, be it a rat, a robot, or a monstrous alien, there will be no welcoming with arms wide open from either side. Again, I'm describing patterns here, not intentional or explicit messages in the movies.

The path to rights and respect from both groups must start with an act of exemplary personhood and humaneness by those who dare to break ranks with their kind. And, thanks to the struggles of the heroes, the Human as Partner story arc ends with a recognition of personhood in the non-human and a huge reward coming to those who accepted the non-humans as fellow persons.

In *Monsters Inc.*, Mike and Sully discover that laughter yields far more energy than screams. In *Ratatouille* Anton

Ego has an epiphany and gives one of my favorite speeches in response to a Proustian flashback he experiences after eating Remy's cooking. In *WALL-E* nothing less than the entire human race is saved from the brink of self-induced extinction. In the world of Pixar, the benefits for humanity are tremendous in every case where non-human persons are treated with respect.

There is one Pixar movie that doesn't fit either the Humans as Antagonists or Humans as Partner structure: *The Incredibles*. Instead of non-human protagonists, we're treated to super-human protagonists and antagonists. Yet the struggle from outcast to redeemer is the same, only this time, it's because the super-humans come together as a family. What enables the Incredible family to succeed is not that they are super-human but that they are humane; that they love, support, and protect one another. As a result, the society that once feared and banished them sees the supers not as Others, but as fellow members of humanity.

Non-Human Liberation

Taken together as a whole narrative, the Pixar canon diagrams what will likely be this century's main rights battle— the rights of personhood for non-humans—in three stages. Again, remember, these are ideas with which an entire generation, just now finding its footing and voice, has been raised.

First are the Humans as Antagonist stories, in which the non-humans discover and develop personhood. I mean, the first work in the Pixar corpus is about Buzz Lightyear, whose character arc is about his becoming self-aware as a toy. These movies represent nascent personhood among non-human entities. For the viewer, we begin to see how some animals and items we see as mindless may have inner lives of which we are unaware.

Second are the Humans as Partners stories, in which exceptional non-humans and exceptional humans share a moment of mutual recognition of personhood. The moment when Linguini realizes Remy is answering him is second only to the moment when Remy shows Ego around the kitchen—such beautiful transformations of the Other into the self. These movies represent the first forays of non-human persons into seeking and achieving parity with human beings.

Third, and finally, there is *The Incredibles*, which turns the personhood equation on its head. Instead of portraying the struggle for non-humans to be accepted as human, *The Incredibles* shows how human enhancement—going *beyond* the human norm—will trigger equally strong reactions of revulsion and otherization. The message, however, is that the human traits we value have nothing to do with our physical powers but are instead based in our moral and emotional bonds and, furthermore, our willingness to *act upon those bonds*. Beneficence and courage require far more humanity than raw might. *The Incredibles* teaches a striking lesson: human enhancement does not make you inhuman—the choices you make and the way you treat others determines how human you really are.

What is staggering here is that Pixar has come closer to properly describing personhood than any philosopher I can think of. Remember, we started this chapter seeing how that task was effectively impossible.

First, through their films, Pixar has covered all the most likely sources of non-human intelligence. For every category there is a character: uplifted animals (Dug), naturally intelligent species (Remy and Kevin), A.I. robots (WALL-E, EVE), and aliens or monsters (Sully and Mike). Then there is the Incredible family, transhumans with superpowers. In telling their stories, Pixar allows these otherwise strange entities to become unmistakably familiar, so clearly akin to us.

Second, these movies show us *how* to identify personhood: Remy's passion for the art of cooking (abstract desire and design); Dug's willingness to disobey orders to protect Kevin and her chicks (recognition of other persons and moral reasoning based on empathy); Mike and Sully's decision to stop scaring kids (recognition of and action to prevent the suffering of others); the Incredibles' heroism (owning the moral responsibilities associated with privilege); WALL-E and EVE's plan to take over the spaceship to return to Earth and to save humanity from itself (do I even need to explain the moral functions at work here?). These movies confront us with *practical* personhood—even without a settled philosophical definition of personhood, would we feel it is ethically acceptable to not grant personhood to individuals that displayed these traits? I doubt it.

The seeds planted by these ideas are already starting to bear fruit. Several recent critically acclaimed and blockbuster films, including *Her*, *Big Hero 6*, and *Interstellar* portray a world in which non-human intelligence (in the case of these three movies, AI) is as ethical as the humans with whom they share the screen. When contrasted with pre-Pixar films (for example, *2001: A Space Odyssey* or *Terminator*), it's worth simply noting that AI in these new movies is portrayed not only as non-malevolent, but as *heroic*, *empathetic*, and capable of *love* in the richest sense. In some moments, the non-human is more ethical than their human counterparts (Baymax, I'm looking at you bud). That these movies have resonated so well with audiences is telling.

As history moves forward and technology with it, these issues will no longer be the imaginings of films and fiction, but of politics and policy. Pixar, however, may have settled the personhood debate before it arrives. By watching our favorite movies, we have been taught that being human is not the same as being a person. And in teaching us how to identify personhood as it comes, Pixar has made it a bit easier for us to bring even more individuals under the big umbrella of rights and responsibilities that come with being a person. We've been shown that new persons and forms of personhood can come from anywhere. Through Pixar, we have opened ourselves up a bit more to a better, more inclusive future.

And therein lies the power of Pixar. For a generation now, we've been shown that humanity does not have a monopoly on personhood. Whatever form non- or super-human intelligence takes, it will need brave souls on both sides to defend it. If we can live up to this burden, humanity and the world we live in will be better for it.

II

The
Troublemaker

5
How Can We Make Entrepreneurs?

STEPHEN R.C. HICKS

As a kid, Steve Jobs hated school. Many of us can relate, even if we're not brilliant business innovators. School bored the young Jobs painfully, and he reacted by engaging in acts of disobedience and defiance. "I was pretty bored in school," he remembers, "and I turned into a little terror." As a result, he was expelled from the third grade. Later, he loathed his junior high school, and one day he simply refused to go back. So adamant was the adolescent Jobs that his parents moved to another California town in hopes of finding a better fit.

The adult Jobs became one of the outstanding entrepreneurs of his generation. But his school experiences raise a question: Did Steve Jobs fail to adapt himself to the system, or did the school system fail to fit Steve Jobs?

A Japanese team of investigators recently came to the United States to study its school system. Japan is a successful nation—prosperous and dynamic in many areas. But the team had a question: *Why does our country have so few innovators?*

They looked to the United States with its many centers of innovation: Silicon Valley technology, Hollywood movies, New York finance, Broadway theater, and others. In the business world, they noted the many entrepreneurs such as Bill Gates, Martha Stewart, Oprah Winfrey, and Mark Zuckerberg.

So the Japanese investigators asked the question: *What are American schools doing so well to generate so many creative, innovative, entrepreneurs?* What's their "secret ingredient"? The question's important, because we live in an era that, for the first time in history, is taking entrepreneurism seriously.

Our business-employment environment is different than it used to be. Steven Rogers has pointed out:

> In the 1960s, 1 out of every 4 persons in the United States worked for a Fortune 500 company. Today, only 1 out of every 14 people works for these companies. Employment at Fortune 500 companies peaked at 16.5 million people in 1979 and has steadily declined every year to approximately 10.5 million people today. (*The Entrepreneur's Guide to Finance and Business*, p. 42)

That's a major shift in the employment market.

Economics has been transforming itself into what economists Arnold Kling and Nick Schulz call "Economics 2.0." For generations, most economists ignored or downplayed the unpredictable and idiosyncratic entrepreneur and focused on abstracted, impersonal models. Contrarians such as Joseph Schumpeter and Israel Kirzner argued for the central importance of entrepreneurship, but they were lonely voices in economics. Only recently has mainstream economics begun recasting itself on the basis of entrepreneurship.

In the Psychology and Ethics literature, we see a movement toward understanding entrepreneurism as key to a flourishing life. Not only in our work but in our overall lives, psychologists like Martin Seligman are stressing autonomy, self-directedness, and creative exploration as foundational ingredients in a healthy life. And moral philosophers are now making connections between entrepreneurial traits and moral virtues in the context of making our careers an integral part of our overall flourishing lives.

So in this new, entrepreneurial century, how do we parents and educators help our children and students prepare for an entrepreneurial economy and an entrepreneurial life?

Asking the Right Question

The Japanese investigators' question is important but misfocused. The American "secret ingredient" is *not* in the schools. Most US formal schooling is government schooling, and most schools are not good at teaching entrepreneurism. Some schools in prosperous neighborhoods are solid, but most are weak and many are terrible.

Consider the many kids who start school full of energy and curiosity and excitement—but after a few years they come to dislike or even hate school. They are bored. They don't like science and they don't even like art. If you ask what their favorite subject is, they'll say it is lunch and recess when they can go outside and play. And for several decades we have seen a decline in test scores and more students graduating with weak reading and math skills and minimal scientific and historical knowledge.

Yet the US does produce a large number of creative individuals. How is this possible?

What American culture does well is what is does *outside* of school. Here I agree with Michael Petrilli. After-school hours are busy with drama and chess clubs and sport and debate teams. American culture also has much parental involvement in music lessons, trips to museums and galleries, sports leagues, summer camps, and travel. And it is prosperous, with much wealth to support informal learning opportunities.

Music education is a good example. Everyone loves music, and American culture has much creativity in music—rock bands, jazz clubs, symphonies in most cities, and more. But that creativity didn't come out of music education in schools. Instead, those who become musicians and music enthusiasts are inspired from popular culture, learning from friends and families, or by lessons paid for by their parents.

All of this points to a challenge for education reform. Schooling currently has two major problems. It wastes much of its students' time, as measured by the students' self-reports of how disengaged they are. And it misses the opportunity to use its considerable resources to prepare young adults for entrepreneurial ideas and living.

Steve Jobs—who, in addition to his troubles in grade school, also dropped out of college—put the entrepreneurial aspiration best:

> Your work is going to fill a large part of your life, and the only way to be truly satisfied is to do what you believe is great work. And the only way to do great work is to love what you do. If you haven't found it yet, keep looking. Don't settle. As with all matters of the heart, you'll know when you find it. And, like any great relationship, it just gets better and better as the years roll on. So keep looking until you find it. Don't settle. (Stanford Commencement Address)

So how can we re-focus the schools to enable students to take on that great life challenge? One element must be educating for entrepreneurship.

The Essentials of Entrepreneurship

The entrepreneurial process begins with an *informed and creative idea* for a new product. The entrepreneur is *ambitious* and *gutsy* and takes the *initiative* in developing the idea into a new enterprise. Through *perseverance* and *trial and error*, the entrepreneur *produces* something of value. He or she takes on a *leadership* role in showing consumers the value of the new product and showing new employees how to make it. The entrepreneur *trades* with them to *win-win* results, thus achieving *success* and *enjoying* its fruits.

Now let's see how each of these italicized terms relates to Steve Jobs.

Entrepreneurs generate business ideas and decide which ones are worth pursuing. In coming up with *informed, creative ideas*, entrepreneurs speak of vision, activeness of mind, and "thinking outside the box." They speak of judgment: Which ideas are actually good ones? Can the product be developed technically? Will it sell? What does the market research show? Entrepreneurs exhibit a commitment to cognitive achievement—intellectual playfulness, research, experimentation, analysis, and judgment. As one venture capitalist put it, "Money does not get the ideas flowing. It's ideas that get the money flowing."

Steve Jobs was characterized by confidence in his creativity and judgment, and he tells us how he acquired it. His parents had moved with the adolescent Jobs to Los Altos, California, near the heart of Silicon Valley. Many of his neighbors were engineers who gathered in garage workshops after work and on weekends to talk and tinker with projects. Jobs's father was a skilled mechanic who liked rebuilding cars in his spare time (*iCon*, p. 10). Across the street lived Steve Wozniak, whose father was an engineer at Hewlett-Packard. And the young Jobs played with do-it-yourself Heathkits. All of that, Jobs explained,

> gave one the sense that one could build things that one saw around oneself in the universe. These things were not mysteries anymore. I mean you looked at a television set, you would think that, 'I haven't built one of those, but I could. There's one of those in the Heathkit catalog and I've built two other Heathkits so I could build that.' Things became much more clear that they were the results of human creation, not these magical things that just appeared in one's environment. . . . It gave a tremendous level of self-confidence, that through exploration and learning one could understand seemingly very complex things. (Quoted in *The Pixar Touch*, p. 76)

Ambition is also characteristic of entrepreneurship—the drive to achieve your goals and be the best that you can be. Many people experience idle wishing—"Wouldn't it be nice if I were rich and independent?" Ambitious individuals feel strongly the *need* to achieve their goals.

Steve Jobs's quest to make his products "insanely great" speaks of a high ambition—and an ambition that embodied a strong integrity. Jobs used the analogy of a carpenter committed to the highest standards of his craft:

When you're a carpenter making a beautiful chest of drawers, you're not going to use a piece of plywood on the back, even though it faces the wall and nobody will ever see it. You'll know it's there, so you're going to use a beautiful piece of wood on the back. For you to sleep well at night, the aesthetic, the quality, has to be carried all the way through. (*Playboy* Interview)

Entrepreneurship requires *initiative*. It's one thing to have a business plan; it's another to turn it into reality. Entrepreneurs are self-starters who commit to bringing their ideas into existence. The teenager Steve Jobs was trying to build a frequency counter but needed some sophisticated parts. So he telephoned Bill Hewlett, co-founder of Hewlett-Packard, at his home. Hewlett didn't know Jobs, but they talked for twenty minutes. Jobs got the parts—as well as a summer job at H-P.

Any entrepreneurial enterprise involves venturing into the unknown, a willingness to take on obstacles, and the possibility of failure. Consequently, entrepreneurship takes *courage*—the willingness to take calculated risks, to be aware of downsides while not letting fear dominate your decision-making.

Courage is closely tied to independence of judgment—not letting pressure from others override your own judgment. One of Jobs's teachers in high school, who taught the school's only course in electronics, noted Steve's independent streak: "He was usually off in a corner doing something on his own and really didn't want to have much of anything to do with me or the rest of the class" (John McCollum, quoted in *iCon*, p. 18).

Jobs himself later put it this way:

Don't be trapped by dogma, which is living the result of other people's thinking. Don't let the noise of other opinions drown your own inner voice. And most important, have the courage to follow your heart and intuition. (Stanford Commencement Address)

Bouncing Back

Success is rarely easy and overnight, so success usually requires sticking with it through difficulties and over the longer term. Entrepreneurs must *persevere* through the technical obstacles, in the face of the naysayers and their own self-doubts. And many entrepreneurs fail several times before achieving success.

The scope and number of Jobs's failures and his ability to bounce back are legendary. The Apple I and II initially sold modestly. The Lisa was a dud. Jobs was then kicked out of Apple. His new company, NeXT, failed. But he tried again, and he tried different approaches, culminating in a return to a struggling Apple. Even then, Jobs had to ask his great rival, Microsoft's Bill Gates, for a $150 million investment. But the persistence paid off, and Jobs proceeded to transform Apple into a global titan—a rejuvenation rightly called (by Jeffrey Young and William Simon) "the greatest second act in the history of business."

Jobs's long-term funding of Pixar also illustrates his perseverance. Pixar's model of digitally-animated movies lost money for years and was kept afloat primarily because Jobs believed in it and continued to fund it. Eventually, Pixar achieved technical and commercial success in movies such as *Toy Story* (1995), *Monsters, Inc.* (2001), and *The Incredibles* (2004).

The entrepreneurial development process is almost always *trial and error*, requiring that the entrepreneur make adjustments based on experience. Successful entrepreneurs respond to real-world feedback and can admit their errors. Steve Jobs's advice to himself and others (quoted by Bob Hill) was "Sometimes when you innovate, you make mistakes. It is best to admit them quickly, and get on with improving your other innovations." Jobs was regularly willing to abandon unsuccessful approaches, and his perfectionism made him require many iterations in product development before, finally, achieving the "insanely great."

Productivity: When the development process culminates in a working product, the entrepreneur has added value to the world. Those who then transact with the entrepreneur, as customers and as employees, engage in *win-win trade*, exchanging value for value. Socially, trade is a process of deal-

59

ing with others on a peaceful basis according to productive merit. The commitment of Apple's customers to their products, sometimes bordering on religious devotion, is a testament to Jobs's and Apple's success at win-win value exchange.

Entrepreneurs also bring *leadership* to the trade. They create something new, so they are the first to go down a new path. Those who go first set an example for others and, especially in the case of something new, they must show customers its value and teach employees how to make it.

Jobs spoke of leadership as a critical component of entrepreneurial success. "Innovation," he liked to say, "distinguishes between a leader and a follower." And, he argued, leadership is the ultimate in human capital: "Innovation has nothing to do with how many R&D [Research and Development] dollars you have. When Apple came up with the Mac, IBM was spending at least 100 times more on R&D. It's not about money. It's about the people you have, how you're led, and how much you get it" (*Fortune*).

Jobs's leadership record is mixed. There are credible accusations that he was often difficult to work with—he could be impatient and throw tantrums, he regularly used verbal abuse to get his way, and he sometimes outright manipulated people. Leaders, especially visionary leaders, have to handle great pressures and deal with less committed and competent people, so handling pressure and people gracefully is a key component of leadership.

Yet there's also Jobs's undeniable track record as a visionary whose charisma attracted many of the best and brightest, with whom he maintained long-term relationships, and whose methods, positive and negative, did motivate people to accomplish much more than they thought possible.

Finally, the entrepreneur experiences *success* and the *enjoyment* of success. Success yields both material and psychic rewards—the goods that money can buy and the experiences of independence and security that go with it. There is also achievement's psychological reward: enhanced self-respect and the sense of accomplishment.

One small anecdote speaks charmingly to Jobs's ability to enjoy his success. In her eulogy for Steve, his sister Mona Simpson tells us: "He told me how much he loved going to the Palo Alto bike store and gleefully realizing he could afford to buy the best bike there. And he did" ("A Sister's Eulogy").

To summarize the above, let's put into a table those traits exhibited by entrepreneurs in general and Jobs in particular:

Entrepreneur Success Trait
Knowledge and creativity
Ambition
Courage
Initiative
Perseverance
Trial and error experimentalism
Productivity
Trade value for value
Leadership
Experiencing and enjoying success

What Schools Could Do

If entrepreneurship involves the exercise of certain traits, where do those traits come from? Can formal schooling instill, develop, or at least enhance those characteristics in students? If we take entrepreneurism as a lens for education, then can we teach creative exploration, courage, initiative, and the other essential qualities?

If we contrast much traditional and current schooling, what do we see? We don't see much uniqueness, activity, or experimentalism. Students sit in straight rows of desks.

They do what the teacher and textbook say. *Every* student does the *same thing* at the *same time* in the *same way* and takes the *same standardized tests*. That is, we see uniformity, obedience, passivity, and rote learning. So while there is useful knowledge in the curriculum, the embedded lessons students also learn are: *Do what the authorities say, Do what everyone else is doing*, and *The correct answers are pre-set and already known*. (And we sometimes wonder why we have so many unmotivated, dependent, and timid students—or students who, out of sheer boredom and the chaotic need to be themselves, rebel in destructive ways.)

So if an explicit goal of education is to cultivate entrepreneurism, as a first step let's consider getting the students out of the rows and letting them interact with prepared materials on their own.

I have three suggestions. One is for us educators to fill in this table with exercises appropriate for children of different ages.

Entrepreneur Success Trait	Educational exercises
Knowledge and creativity	
Ambition	
Courage	
Initiative	
Perseverance	
Trial and error	
Productivity	
Trade value for value	
Leadership	
Experiencing and enjoying success	

Take courage as one example.

Courage is the virtue of acting as you judge best despite fear. Fear comes in many forms—of pain, of disapproval, of feeling like a failure, of loss of love, money, and so on. Life involves many risks, so having the character to handle risk is an important part of success. One direct connection to entrepreneurship is the many people who do not attempt it due to fear.

So one thread within entrepreneurial education is to develop formal exercises that embody risk and help a child learn to manage it.

Younger children learn skills that involve *physical* risks: going down a slide, jumping into a pool, learning to ride a bicycle. Such activities and dozens more can be formally identified and introduced in schools as exercises. They can also be scaled up as children mature. Eventually, they will be able to handle mixing chemicals, climbing rock-walls, and driving cars.

Other risks are more *psychological*. For younger children, these can include greeting and conversing with new adults whom your parents have invited for dinner, raising your hand to ask the teacher a question, or expressing an opinion different than your classmates'. Again, exercises to model these can be introduced and scaled up as children mature so that eventually they can handle giving a speech before a large audience, asking someone for a date, and arguing civilly about political and religious differences.

And what holds for developing courage also holds for developing initiative, experimentalism, perseverance, and the other success traits.

A second possibility is to explore further the Montessori approach to education. Maria Montessori opened her first school in Rome in 1907, and for over a century her method has spread, mostly as a grassroots phenomenon, all over the world. The scholarly literature is beginning to study Montessori's results systematically and to judge them positively, but for now let's note two indicators.

Anecdotally, Montessori advocates note that four leading entrepreneurs of our generation—Larry Page and Sergey Brin of Google, Jeff Bezos of Amazon, and Jimmy Wales of

Wikipedia—were Montessori-educated ("Google Founders Talk Montessori").

More formally, Hal Gregersen reports a striking statistic. After interviewing a large number of entrepreneurs, Gregersen notes:

> It's fascinating when we interview these famous entrepreneurs to realise that they grew up in worlds where adults paid attention to these innovation skills. Most often these adults were parents and grandparents, but in about *one-third* of the cases they were master teachers at Montessori or Montessori-like schools. (Quoted by Nicholas Bray, italics added)

A third option is to learn from supplemental programs that explicitly tie education to entrepreneurship. Two examples are the Network for Teaching Entrepreneurship (NFTE) and Junior Achievement (JA), both with many chapters in the US and other countries.

Steve Mariotti, founder of NFTE, began teaching at one of New York City's worst public schools. He used traditional methods but found that they failed to teach the students anything. Then he realized that children, especially poor kids, are often fascinated with money but know nothing about how to make it. So, using his own entrepreneurial experience, Mariotti changed his methods and explicitly began teaching students how to start their own businesses. Their attitudes altered dramatically. Their profit motive kicked in, and they began to see a realistic potential for a better life. Thinking about business led them to see the need for other skills—reading, writing, math, and social—and they became motivated to learn from their textbooks and other teachers. Students in Junior Achievement have achieved similar results in Argentina, as reported by Eduardo Marty.

Dirt Bikes and Dads

How many children with Steve-Jobs potential have been stifled by anti-entrepreneurial schooling? How many future entrepreneurs creating insanely great things could be nurtured by a re-focused, entrepreneurial education?

Beyond that, let's not overlook the role that parents can play. Here's something I observed in my own neighborhood, which I think captures the heart of education.

On my drive home from work I passed regularly some vacant land upon which kids with their bikes had created paths and piles of dirt to jump over. Over time, their efforts became more elaborate. They built crude ramps with wood (likely stolen from nearby construction sites), dug shallow pits and let them fill with water, and extended the crisscrossing network of riding paths. I confess to some envy—being a middle-aged man who wanted again to be a kid out there riding my bike up the ramps and jumping the puddles.

But what really caught my attention was an evening when there was suddenly much more activity at the dirt bike site. The fathers had gotten involved. So I stopped my truck and went to watch. The ramps were now sturdier, and the activity was organized. Kids with bikes were lined up at one end of a long stretch of path, and each kid would ride his or her bike fast up and over the ramp and fly through the air as far as possible.

That wasn't all. One of the dads had a radar gun that measured how fast each kid's bike was going when it hit the ramp. Another dad, working with one of the kids, measured the distance of each jump and recorded it in a notebook. And all of the kids were now wearing helmets. But each kid wanted to know how far he had jumped, how to improve his distance, and as they waited their turns they were discussing the best air pressures for the tires, bike speeds and ramp angles, lubrication for their bike's gears, and more.

The point for entrepreneurial education is that the kids first showed initiative and pursued their interests. The adults got involved and both encouraged that initiative and facilitated a more structured activity. The kids were learning math and engineering, co-operation and competition, being creative and getting exercise—and having a whole lot of fun themselves and with their dads.

That's just one story, though it points to a path for entrepreneurial educators to pursue. What some kids and their dads can do with a vacant lot and some creativity—we professional educators with our training and resources should be able to do even better.

6
The Visionary Entrepreneur

ROBERT F. SALVINO

His tale is thus both instructive and cautionary, filled with lessons about innovation, character, leadership, and values.

—WALTER ISAACSON, *Steve Jobs*, p. xxi

Entrepreneurs are risk-takers, profit-seekers. We can never identify who will be the next great entrepreneur, or what will be the next great product. You might have a strong feeling about one particular person you know or may have encountered or one particular thing you have envisioned or even held in your hands, but collectively we can't know. Innovators, profitable enterprises, and their valued products are random occurrences emerging from the spontaneous order of the market process.

Steve Jobs was an entrepreneur of a very exclusive class. He was a billionaire. According to research by Sanandaji and Leeson, there were 234 billionaires in the United States in 2009, comprising just 0.00008 percent of the population. Almost no one actually knows a billionaire; fewer still can claim to know one well. Today many do claim to know a great deal about Steve Jobs, his reputation as a jerk, his quirky habits. His products are almost everywhere, and because of his products we have access to more information about Steve Jobs than we have ever had about entrepreneurs in the past.

Many would describe Steve Jobs as an egoist, and that's probably right. He was an entrepreneur, a capitalist, an individualist. Very few people seem to routinely follow their own self-interest as a matter of course, even fewer as ruthlessly as Steve Jobs reportedly did. But as a class, entrepreneurs in general may be more likely than most to pursue their interests unwaveringly. Successful people in general are focused on their goals, and this focus requires an independent, seemingly self-absorbed approach to life. We're familiar with the stories of dedicated practice of great athletes like Tiger Woods and Kobe Bryant, and we're also familiar with the hardships in their personal and professional relationships. The same can be said of musicians. Iconic musical groups that have lasted for decades are extremely rare. More often we hear the stories of the break-ups, the personal, irreconcilable differences.

That we have such reverence for the achievements of people like this, yet so many express a sense of relief or sometimes even snicker at their failures, is a great irony. These fanatically driven achievers make other people uncomfortable. To paraphrase Jobs's hand-picked biographer, Walter Isaacson, their personalities, passions, and achievements are all inter-related. He said this of Steve Jobs, but he could have been describing any successful entrepreneur or innovative artist. Their dedication could be viewed as "over-the-top" and most people can only handle so much of them. Many might like them to turn it down a notch, take a break, live a little, and join the rest of us for a while, but if they did we would likely never know of their achievements and neither would they.

Adam Smith didn't promote self-interest per se, but he maintained that it is an entrepreneur's pursuit of his own self-interest, rather than anyone's good intentions, that best ensures the satisfaction of people's wants. Ralph Waldo Emerson heralded self-reliance and integrity to our own thoughts so that we may fulfill our truest desires uncorrupted by the will of others. Ayn Rand crowned selfishness as a virtue and proclaimed its sole measure is man's unrelenting pursuit of his own ideal. The validity of these notions is evidenced in our regard for the entrepreneur, the independent soul who undertakes risk to will his thoughts into actions, thus standing for himself of his own accord.

These independent, ambitious traits are the wellsprings of progress. The entrepreneur's drive to build a better mousetrap, in pursuit of profit, ultimately allows the rest of us to enjoy greater variety in our lives, to get more and better goods and services out of our earned dollars, to work less yet still produce more.

The Entrepreneur as Destroyer

'Creative destruction' is Joseph Schumpeter's artful term describing how the marketplace responds to an innovation that brings into being a better product, service, or method. On economic grounds it is better because it is more efficient, consuming fewer resources for a greater result. In so doing, however, it makes the existing technology inferior.

Take the automobile. It gets us from point A to point B with greater ease and comfort, and with far less pollution than the thing it replaced—the horse and carriage. Think of the problem of disposing of horse manure in a large city congested with horse and carriage traffic. Imagine the rain washing over the dung heaps—a common method of storing the build-up of waste from the horses—and then the sun drying the heaps and the wind blowing the dung dust throughout the city and the rain bringing the dust to the ground again, layering everything with a coating of dung. (This historical story was vividly illustrated in a guest lecture by Professor Brad Hobbs, delivered to my classes at Coastal Carolina University in 2013.)

The automobile solved this and many other problems. It also called for more and better roads as thousands of places suddenly came within a day's drive by car—opening the world and all of its possibilities to millions of people previously shut out from the pathways of progress. This new development disrupted everything and everyone associated with the horse and carriage industry. The innovation of the automobile eventually brought about the destruction of the horse and carriage industry. Schumpeter identified "creative destruction" as the fundamental driving force of capitalist progress.

The creative and destructive forces are resisted by some, either for immediate financial motives, from fear, or from lack of understanding, lack of foresight, or just an unwillingness to adapt to change. The Hewlett Packard executives didn't feel the new desktop created by Steve Wozniak, an employee of HP at the time, fit into the core vision of HP. Fortunately for Wozniak he was already associating with a group of young innovators willing to take risks. A collectivist ethic would have hindered Wozniak from developing and marketing his computer because this would, if successful, have disrupted the current state of affairs, but the economic freedom inherent in pure capitalism enabled Wozniak to take his ideas elsewhere, to form his own company, and undertake risk for his own gain or loss. His friend Steve Jobs saw the commercial appeal and the two began producing crude desktop computers in Jobs's garage in the 1970s, reminiscent of the way Hewlett and Packard had begun their technology company in the 1930s.

Pursuing His Own Vision

Steve Jobs showed an affinity for technology early in life. His adopted father made side money purchasing used vehicles and refurbishing them to sell on the used market. He taught Steve some of the basics of mechanics and electronics and also the way of turning a dollar into two with a little resourcefulness. According to many accounts Steve was building a frequency counter in eighth grade for a school project and needed parts. He looked up the phone number for Bill Hewlett, co-founder of Hewlett Packard, and made a direct call, an action that most people would never have had the courage or will to take. He spoke directly with Bill Hewlett and several days later walked into the offices of HP and received a bag full of parts personally assembled by Bill Hewlett. This was Palo Alto in the late 1960s. That summer Steve was given a job at Hewlett Packard, something child labor laws would prevent today.

Apple combined the engineering and marketing genius of Wozniak and Jobs. We often hear that the company they launched would go on to revolutionize six, maybe seven, entire industries—personal desktop computers, laptops, tablets, smartphones, music distribution, portable music players, and possibly even retail stores. This is a broad characterization and ignores such obvious technologies as photography and videography. It also ignores the use of apps to bring thousands upon thousands of features to our fingertips with a simple, quick download. Everything from compasses to guitar tuners to GPS navigation can be downloaded to a smartphone with an app. New product and service apps are entering the marketplace every day.

iProfit—uBenefit

Steve Jobs had a vision to create "insanely great" products and ultimately to build a company that would stand tall even in his absence. By most measures he achieved the former, but the latter remains to be seen. His first absence from the company, arguably forced by the board of directors, saw Apple decline, almost into bankruptcy, only to be revived by the return of Jobs twelve years later and the return of his crude approach to management and stellar gains in the company's valuation.

Jobs placed quality on a pedestal—above character, above reputation, above profit maximization. The quality he demanded and protected was truly a quality of his own design and purpose. He demanded total control and sometimes the features resulting would come to be viewed as less favorable to consumers, but Jobs was unyielding. He demanded quality the way he envisioned it.

Steve Jobs's approach would have pleased William Edwards Deming, the father of quality management. Deming's philosophy of quality management, developed in the 1920s through the 1940s, was adopted by Japanese firms in the 1950s. Up to that point, Japanese manufacturers had been chiefly noted for their cheap, inferior copies of Western designs. Deming's system of thinking about management led to the paradoxical conclusion: If you focus on quality, then quality will rise and costs will fall, but if you focus on costs, costs will rise and quality will fall. Many corporations appear to have this backwards, but at least for a time with Jobs at the helm, Apple had it right.

He wasn't merely trying to please the customer. Steve Jobs believed no one knew what was best for the consumer as well as he, Steve Jobs, did. He was like *Seinfeld*'s "Soup Nazi," and there are still lines out the door of Apple stores whenever a new product hits the shelves. If the customers don't like it, there's plenty of competition (I am writing this on a Dell laptop and my phone of choice is a Google Android device, but my music comes from iTunes, and I play it on an iPod).

All of this is not to suggest that theories of self-interest or egoism simply advocate doing things your way—not if your way just isn't very good. Jobs believed that his way was beyond the best the customer could conceive, and he and his team at Apple delivered. No amount of market research could persuade Steve Jobs that his intuition was not right. He believed in the power of his own mind over the power of objective analysis of existing conditions.

> Some people say, "Give the customers what they want." But that's not my approach. Our job is to figure out what they're going to want before they do. I think Henry Ford once said, "If I'd asked customers what they wanted, they would have told me, 'A faster horse!'" People don't know what they want until you show it to them. That's why I never rely on market research. Our task is to read things that are not yet on the page. (Walter Isaacson, *Steve Jobs,* p. 567)

Jobs has been compared to the heroes of Ayn Rand's novels. Luskin and Greta's book, *I Am John Galt,* devotes a chapter to Steve Jobs, portraying him as the real life Howard

Roark—Ayn Rand's individualist architect from *The Fountainhead*. But my conversations with philosophy professors acquainted with Rand's thinking suggest that the intuitive approach of Jobs was extremely *un*-Randian. Jobs was less likely to rely on reason, the cornerstone of Rand's philosophy, than on his own intuitive grasp. However, Jobs comes as close to a Rand character as any known businessman ever has when considering two other virtues of her philosophy— the virtues of *independence* and *integrity*. Rand described *independence* as accepting the responsibility to form your own judgments and to live by the work of your own mind and *integrity* as the responsibility to never sacrifice your own convictions to the opinions, will, or wishes of others. It seems Jobs deserved an A+ for those qualities.

Marketing consultants warn against everyone adopting Jobs's approach. After all, most people simply don't know as much about their craft as Jobs knew about his or have access to the best talent in the world to help try to put their *crazy* thoughts into action. When Jobs made the comments quoted above he already had almost twenty years of direct experience in his field and had already been at the helm of one of history's most innovative companies for nearly a decade. So it may not be entirely accurate to suppose that Jobs didn't rely on rational thought. He may just have been genius enough to know that *his* reason was objective and that his famous "reality distortion field" was in fact based on his own rational calculations—regardless of whether others thought they were realistic.

Ethical Lapses

If an entrepreneur and his business get big enough and last long enough, even for the great ones, criticism and controversy will find its way into their stories. Steve Jobs and Apple have come under fire for three main reasons: allegedly unjust exploitation of labor in poor countries, Jobs's harsh verbal treatment of his subordinates, and his seemingly niggardly approach to charitable giving.

The biggest source of controversy associated with Steve Jobs and Apple has been the succession of news stories and protests about the bad working conditions at Foxconn factories in China. Foxconn is the biggest private employer in China, with a million employees. It is a contract manufacturer for all the major western makers of electronic appliances, including Apple.

Foxconn's factories have been described as 'labor camps' and the conditions compared with slavery. Wages are low and a twelve-hour day is common. Allegations were made that suicides occurred because of the poor conditions, though it was later found that suicides among Foxconn employees are lower than in China as a whole (which has a high suicide rate), and even lower than the suicide rate in the United States.

There's a huge difference between general conditions and institutions in China and the US, though the difference in conditions gets slightly less each year. Although Chinese productivity and incomes are rising rapidly—partly because of the employment generated by companies like Apple through contractors like Foxconn—China is still far behind the US in productivity and therefore in income and customary workplace standards.

To make an accurate comparison of real incomes across different countries, economists at the International Monetary Fund use a special measure called Geary-Khamis dollars. By this measure in 2013, the United States ranked number six of all countries in the world at $53,101 per head, while China ranked number ninety-three at $9,844 per head. On average US citizens have over five times the annual income (per person) of Chinese citizens. The US Census shows that the richest state in the US in 2012, Connecticut, had an income per head of $59,687, while the poorest state, Mississippi, had an income of $33,657 per head. So the average resident of poor Mississippi was almost four times richer than the average resident of China.

This is not to say that Apple doesn't have a moral obligation to confront the issue, and to its credit it has. Apple has insisted on audits of pay and working conditions, leading to substantial pay increases and workplace improvements, though pay and conditions are currently, of course, still way behind those in the West. Furthermore, political conditions limit what outside investors can do. In the short run Apple can only go so far in persuading firms in China to improve the working environment. Business freedom has increased in China in recent decades, yet the Communist Party maintains strong controls over speech, labor, and industry. In the words of the Global Economy Rankings on Economic Freedom, "The Communist Party's ultimate authority throughout the economic system undermines the rule of law, and institutionalized cronyism remains pervasive" (Heritage.org 2014).

The second complaint concerns the harsh treatment or verbal lashings Jobs unleashed on those whose ideas he didn't accept or whose work he didn't deem up to his standards. This is a difficult one to analyze because we're forced to look at the complaints of some without knowing all the relevant circumstances. One noteworthy account comes from his ex-wife in her own book on Steve Jobs. That probably isn't the least biased source. There are those who didn't receive the treatment so criticized by others, at least those who didn't consider it significant enough to place it above all other aspects of his character. He was a CEO, and even before that he was a leader on a path destined to high achievement. This also doesn't excuse his treatment of others, but it does suggest the intensity of his relationships was far beyond the typical relationships even in business. Even among business leaders, most don't regard their work with the intensity of someone like Steve Jobs. Another possible explanation for the numerous stories of harsh treatment may be that his management style seemed to keep him in the operations side of the business more than most CEOs. He was approachable, exposed to more personalities. All in all, it appears that Jobs displayed more anger than he ought to have done.

Steve Jobs held an unpopular view of philanthropy. His actions were also unpopular. He didn't join Bill Gates and

Warren Buffett in their pledge to give away most of their fortunes. He wasn't actively involved with his wife's foundations. He didn't get behind their missions in public speaking opportunities or site visits. He actually did set up a foundation of his own in the 1980s and became very frustrated with the whole thing. According to Caroline Preston, writing for the online *Chronicle of Philanthropy*, Jobs found "professional philanthropy—the jargon, showiness, and all the rich people who thought they could shake it up—distasteful." Some of his views come from his initial experience with this foundation.

Perhaps the best defense of his position on philanthropy comes from a conversation he had with Walter Isaacson while working on his biography. According to Isaacson as reported by Ullekh, Jobs said he "would be able to do more to reform education, for example, by creating an iPad that had interactive textbooks than by being a philanthropist giving his money away." This is consistent with the view put forth by philosopher Stephen Hicks. Entrepreneurs can do the most for society by focusing their efforts on creating the greatest products for the most people. (For more on Jobs and charity, see Chapter 9 in this volume.)

Entrepreneurship allows us to have more with the use of less resources; it reduces the prices of goods and services, thus enabling more people to benefit. An iPad may seem expensive relative to a book, but the iPad enables access to an infinite trove of information and exploration, so in real terms the iPad has reduced the cost of acquiring information, and hopefully knowledge—but that is up to the user. A philosophy of business ethics that would make a Steve Jobs divert his resources and talents away from his chosen entrepreneurial pursuit would be inefficient on economic grounds.

On philosophical grounds, it would infringe upon his pursuit of his own virtue. It would corrupt him. It's better to leave the choice open and let others more so inclined pursue that path, their path, not the path of Steve Jobs.

7
But Steve Jobs Didn't Invent Anything!

RYAN KRAUSE AND OWEN PARKER

In October of 2011, *The New York Times* published an obituary of Steve Jobs, heralding him as a "visionary who . . . helped usher in the era of personal computers and then led a cultural transformation in the way music, movies and mobile communications were experienced in the digital age."

Others have lauded him as one of the greatest innovators and entrepreneurs of the late twentieth and early twenty-first centuries, on a par with Henry Ford, Alexander Graham Bell, and Thomas Edison. Almost as often, however, Jobs's critics argue that his merits in these roles are overstated because his products (such as the Apple computer, the iPod, or the iPhone) were not new technologies when he introduced them, but were simply integrations of existing technologies.

Because of this—so these critics argue—the products that Jobs introduced and the company he built around them do not constitute a great achievement. Factually speaking, these critics are not wrong; in almost all cases Jobs's products did not constitute never-before-seen technological advancements. Even within Apple, Jobs's initial role was not uniquely technical, according to an early employee, Avi Solomon: "Between Woz [co-founder Steve Wozniak] and Jobs, Woz was the innovator, the inventor. Steve Jobs was the marketing person."

But are Jobs's critics right in their evaluation of this fact? Did Steve Jobs simply get rich off the ingenuity of others, and therefore not deserve the designation of great innovator and entrepreneur? Were his innovations not nearly as valuable as people think, and valuable to whom?

To answer these questions, we draw on novelist-philosopher Ayn Rand's objective theory of value. Rand rejected what she called the intrinsic and subjective theories of value. The intrinsic theory of value "holds that the good is inherent in certain things or actions as such, regardless of their context and consequences, regardless of any benefit or injury they may cause to the actors and subjects involved"; the subjective theory of value "holds that the good bears no relation to the facts of reality, that it is the product of man's consciousness" ("What Is Capitalism," pp. 13–14). In contrast, Rand's objective theory rejects both the intrinsic and subjective perspectives, and "holds that the good is neither an attribute of 'things in themselves' nor of man's emotional states, but *an evaluation* of the facts of reality by man's consciousness according to a rational standard of value."

Rand defines value as "that which man acts to gain and/or keep", and she argues that the concept "presupposes an answer to the question: of value to whom and for what" ("The Objectivist Ethics," p. 15). According to the objective theory of economic value, therefore, a product or service is only said to be "valuable" in light of its meaningful and empirically verifiable *utility* for human life. Its value is not left up entirely to the opinion of whoever might attempt to evaluate it.

In order to determine a product or service's value, individuals must assess the contribution a product or service makes to the furtherance of their own lives, because values "cannot exist (cannot be valued) outside the full context of a man's life, needs, goals, and knowledge." According to Rand, it's through this process that the valuation of products and services can and must be objective, "determined by the nature of reality, but to be discovered by man's mind." At first glance, the intrinsic and subjective theories of value might seem like straw men arguments that Rand set up to be refuted by her own theory. These theories, however, underpin most of the criticism of Steve Jobs and entrepreneurs in his mold.

For instance, someone operating on an intrinsic theory of value might argue that technologies, once created, have a set value that is inherent to that technology, regardless of how—or whether—it is used. Many critics of Steve Jobs insist that he did not actually invent the technologies his company sold, but merely capitalized on their pre-existing value; he was simply good at being "in the right place at the right time." Such critics insist that the value of a technology exists in the thing itself prior to any recognition—or recombination—of the technology. Recognition of value and recombination of technology comprise Jobs's primary contribution to his products.

On the other side of the coin, someone operating on a subjective theory of value might argue that the value of a technology is entirely arbitrary, and thus by taking existing technologies and transforming them into high-end consumer products, Jobs artificially "created" the value that customers ascribe to his products, with subjective customer opinions constituting the entirety of a product's market value. Subjective value theorists would likely insist that Jobs's success is attributable not to the provision of objective value to his customers, but rather to his ability to trick his customers into paying more than needed for a given technology.

These competing criticisms both build on the same false dichotomy, according to Rand. Economic value is neither an inherent quality of reality nor a subjective whim. This does not mean, however, that Jobs's critics are inventing a tension where none exists; they clearly perceive some difference between the activities of an inventor and a marketer, but their epistemological conclusions are off-base. Value—or entrepreneurial opportunities, depending on the focus of scholarship—is objective, in that individuals must use facts to assess a product or service's utility in the context of their own lives. Moreover, the tension that most people recognize between the inventor and the marketer exists not between intrinsic and subjective value, but rather between two kinds of *objective* value: what Rand labeled "philosophically objective value" and "socially objective value."

Philosophically objective value refers to "a value estimated from the standpoint of the best possible to man, i.e., by the criterion of the most rational mind possessing the greatest knowledge, in a given category, in a given period, and in a defined context." As a point of comparison, we might argue that a number of personal computers on the market were technologically superior to the iMac when Apple introduced it in 1998; there were products with greater computing power, storage, memory, customizability, or other benefits. So it could reasonably be argued that the iMac was not *the* leading edge in terms of its ability to enhance human life in the abstract. In fact, it was priced reasonably low and even positioned, according to Paul Thurrott, as an "internet-age computer for the rest of us."

Despite the fact that the iMac's primary innovation was not in driving forward the frontier of human computing ability, but rather to "bring up the rear" through ease-of-use, sales of the iMac proved so robust that most observers today credit it with raising Apple out of the corporate ashes and enabling the later creation of the iPod, the iPhone, and the iPad. What explains this success in the absence of ground-breaking technological advancement? The answer lies in Rand's concept of socially objective value, defined as "the sum of the individual judgments of all the men involved in trade at a given time, the sum of what they valued, each in the context of his own life" ("What Is Capitalism?", p. 17).

In other words, an individual might objectively determine that a competing personal computer is more valuable to human life in the abstract than is the iMac, and simultaneously objectively determine that the iMac is more beneficial to *him* in the context of his own life, perhaps because he has no material use for the added functionality of the other device or because his degree of technological acumen requires a product that is easier to use. As Rand explains:

> Just as the number of its adherents is not a proof of an idea's truth or falsehood, of an art work's merit or demerit, of a product's efficacy or inefficacy—so the free-market value of goods or services does not necessarily represent their philosophically objective value, but only their *socially objective* value.
>
> Thus, a manufacturer of lipstick may well make a greater fortune than a manufacturer of microscopes—even though it can be rationally demonstrated that microscopes are scientifically more valuable than lipstick. But—valuable to whom?
>
> A microscope is of no value to a little stenographer struggling to make a living; a lipstick is; a lipstick, to her, may mean the difference between self-confidence and self-doubt, between glamour and drudgery. ("What Is Capitalism," p. 17)

Rand hastens to point out that socially objective value is not subjective; individuals (for the most part) evaluate products and services by the real-world results the individuals expect from them. Nevertheless, real though these results are, they occur within the context of individual lives, and thus the value a particular individual derives from a product may differ significantly from its philosophically objective value.

The distinction between philosophically objective value and socially objective value forms the basis for what we see as one of the most fundamental epistemological processes inherent in entrepreneurial activity. The process consists of two basic steps. First, the entrepreneur must identify in a product or service sufficient philosophically objective value such that he or she could potentially profit from selling it. Such identification can occur through the entrepreneur's invention and subsequent evaluation of a wholly new technology, through the determination of an existing technology's value to human life, or through some mixture of the two.

Second, the entrepreneur must create socially objective value from the technology he or she has identified as having philosophically objective value. The entrepreneur can create such value through transforming the existing technology in a useful way, by demonstrating the technology's value to potential customers, or by applying the technology in a more operationally effective fashion. According to Rand,

> The majority learn by demonstration, the minority are free to demonstrate. The 'philosophically objective' value of a new product serves as the teacher for those who are willing to exercise their rational faculty, each to the extent of his ability. ("What Is Capitalism?", p. 18)

When the epistemology of entrepreneurship is conceptualized in this way, it's clear that inventing a new technology, while certainly not inconsistent with the process, is neither a necessary nor a sufficient condition of entrepreneurship. The role of the inventor is to create a product with philosophically objective value. While undeniably important, such scientific discovery and subsequent technological development does not constitute entrepreneurship, and does not guarantee that the technology will be widely adopted or achieve market success. Failure to fully transform a product with philosophically objective value into a product with socially objective value has proven the downfall of countless would-be entrepreneurs.

Steve Jobs understood the epistemology of entrepreneurship and executed it with precision and foresight. Steve Jobs did not invent the personal computer—if anyone associated with Apple could be considered to have played a role in inventing the personal computer, it would be Steve Wozniak—but Jobs saw a potential for socially objective value in its use that no one else in the technology industry could see.

Xerox's PARC developed the technology for the mouse-driven graphical user interface, but it was Jobs who demonstrated the value of these inventions to the general public and thereby monetized them, first through the Lisa operating system and subsequently through the introduction of the Macintosh computer. The same can be said of mp3 player technology and smartphone technology; the former vis-à-vis the iPod, and both vis-à-vis the iPhone. In the field of innovation management, adopters of technology are categorized by Everett Rogers with respect to the timing of adoption: innovators, early adopters, early majority, late adopters, and laggards. Technologies achieve a critical mass of adoption when early adopters give way to the early majority. Steve Jobs's influence can be seen in the creation of early majorities for almost every consumer electronic device developed in the last half century.

Contrary to the claims of the subjectivists and those who argue that entrepreneurial opportunities exist only in the mind of the entrepreneur, the market value that Steve Jobs was able to generate from his products derived from his ability to demonstrate their socially *objective* value. Jobs's marketing skills did not amount to tricking people into buying his products out of momentary deviations from rationality. That type of sales tactic might sustain short-term sales of a fad product, but not the fierce, decades-long customer loyalty that Apple enjoyed under Jobs and continues to enjoy after his passing.

Rather, Jobs fashioned his innovations—yes, built using others' technological inventions—according to what his independent judgment determined to be the most value to the early majority and late adopters. Attributes such as ease-of-use rarely factored into early technological designs of personal computers and smartphones, because the intended users—early adopters—possessed the technological acumen to use complicated devices. Jobs understood the socially objective value in providing easy-to-use products to the majority of uninitiated device users.

In an interview with *Inc.* magazine, which named him "Entrepreneur of the Decade" in 1989, Jobs emphasized the role of objectively assessing a technology's value, both from an abstract as well as from a social standpoint, as opposed to catering to customers' subjective whims. When asked where great products come from, he replied:

> I think really great products come from melding two points of view—the technology point of view and the customer point of view.

You need both. You can't just ask customers what they want and then try to give that to them. By the time you get it built, they'll want something new . . .

. . . customers can't anticipate what the technology can do. They won't ask for things that they think are impossible. But the technology may be ahead of them. If you happen to mention something, they'll say, "Of course, I'll take that. Do you mean I can have that, too?" It sounds logical to ask customers what they want and then give it to them. But they rarely wind up getting what they really want that way . . .

You can get into just as much trouble by going into the technology lab and asking your engineers, "Okay, what can you do for me today?" That rarely leads to a product that customers want or to one that you're very proud of building when you get done. You have to merge these points of view, and you have to do it in an interactive way over a period of time—which doesn't mean a week. It takes a long time to pull out of customers what they really want, and it takes a long time to pull out of technology what it can really give. (Bo Burlingham and George Gendron, "The Entrepreneur of the Decade")

Ayn Rand might as well have been writing about Steve Jobs when she observed that "the free market is not ruled by the intellectual criteria of the majority, which prevail only at and for any given moment; the free market is ruled by those who are able to see and plan long-range—and the better the mind, the longer the range" ("What Is Capitalism," p. 19).

The workings of Steve Jobs's mind epitomized the epistemology of entrepreneurship. He was able to understand the philosophically objective value of new technologies *and* to demonstrate the socially objective value of the products derived from those technologies better than anyone else in the industry (see Xerox's management of PARC inventions). According to Rand, he therefore deserves not only the material wealth that sales of his products generated for him, but also, and perhaps more importantly, the praise and admiration of all of us who use and enjoy those products today. Whether or not the technology behind personal computers, mp3 players, and smartphones had ever been invented, we might not benefit from them as much or even at all were it not for the entrepreneurial epistemology of Steve Jobs.

8
What Does Market Success Show?

WILLIAM R THOMAS

Steve Jobs may never have produced a bad product. He was an obsessive stickler for quality and beauty. Although he was not an engineer and never designed and built a product alone, he insisted that the products he oversaw be integrated, elegant, and eminently usable. His products were very often successful in the marketplace too: they sold well, at a profit. As we'll see, when he was associated with products that didn't sell, usually he wasn't actually responsible for those projects.

Is market success the measure of a good product? Were the Apple II and the iPod great products regardless of how they sold, or do we say they were great because they sold well?

Quality and Success

You may think that whether a product succeeds in the market has nothing much to do with real quality. Aren't buyers bamboozled by advertising? Steve Jobs was a master at marketing, as can been seen in the famous "Big Brother" ad that launched the Macintosh, in the "Think Different" campaign of the 1990s, or in Jobs's famous product reveal presentations of the iPod and iPhone. And yes, Jobs himself played a huge role in each of those ad campaigns: vetting ads, designing the event, demanding changes, and even writing copy.

But market success is itself a standard by which we commonly judge quality. Warren Buffett is hailed as the "sage of Omaha" because, fundamentally, he is one of the most successful investors of the past fifty years. The shareholders in his company have made a lot of money investing with Buffett. And his success basically consists in identifying investments that other people will later come to value. There are plenty of investors who can write folksy nostrums, as Buffett does in the Berkshire Hathaway annual report. But no one is regarded as a successful investor simply on the basis of the quality of his nostrums.

And something similar was very much true of Steve Jobs. Jobs is regarded as a brilliant entrepreneur because he was instrumental in the creation of popular products, from the Apple II (Apple's first mass-market computer); to the Macintosh (which was the first successful computer with a graphical user interface); to *Toy Story* and a string of Pixar computer animated movie hits; to the iPod, the iPhone, and the iPad. Throughout his career, Steve Jobs didn't merely orchestrate the creation of products that experts regarded as good, but also created products that generated substantial profits.

In fact, very few of Steve Jobs's products were not commercially successful. In Jobs's first tenure at Apple, from 1975 to 1985, he directly oversaw the Apple I, the Apple II, and the Macintosh, all successes in the marketplace. (When Jobs oversaw a project, he typically exerted an obsessive level of control over all aspects from engineering, to design, to manufacturing, to marketing.)

During that period, the other notable Apple computers were the Lisa and the Apple III, neither of which were commercial or critical successes. Although Jobs had some involvement in both those products—he named the Lisa, for example—he did not control the final design or engineering decisions for either, despite being the marketing face of Apple at the time. For his part, Jobs attributed the market failure of the Lisa to bad design and engineering decisions that compromised its cost and quality (*Steve Jobs*, pp. 101, 181). For

Jobs, success in the marketplace was what he expected to see if he had succeeded in creating a great product.

The most notable example of a Jobs failure is NeXT, the computer company Jobs founded after being ejected from Apple in 1985. NeXT's workstations were produced from 1989 to 1993 and perhaps fifty thousand were sold total. NeXT computers were beautiful, with spare black lines. Their operating systems incorporated advanced technology, such as object-oriented programming, which has since become ubiquitous. The first World Wide Web server ran on a NeXT.

While it was not highly profitable, Jobs was able to sell NeXT to Apple at the end of 1996, ensuring that the investors were compensated, and Jobs brought many NeXT staff members to Apple when he took charge of Apple again in 1997. The NeXT operating system contributed components of Apple's hugely popular new operating systems, OSX and iOS. But compared to his Apple products, or to the Pixar movies, NeXT was a financial disappointment. Certainly, it never reached a broad and sustainable market. Its failure made the world ask whether Steve Jobs was washed up as a technological innovator.

Another example of Jobs failing in the marketplace was the Power Mac G4 Cube (*Steve Jobs*, pp. 444–46). The G4 Cube was an instance of the highly stylish designs that Jobs oversaw at Apple after his return, created in co-operation with the designer Jonathan Ive. It was a smooth, rounded white cube eight inches to a side. It would be featured in a display at the Museum of Modern Art in New York City—a sign of the esteem the minimalist design won among art critics. Jobs's biographer Walter Isaacson describes it like so:

> The G4 Cube was almost ostentatious in its lack of ostentation, and it was powerful. But it was not a success. It had been designed as a high-end desktop, but Jobs wanted to turn it, as he did almost every product, into something that could be mass-marketed to consumers. The Cube ended up not serving either market well. Workaday professionals weren't seeking a jewel-like sculpture for their

desks, and mass-market consumers were not eager to spend twice
what they'd pay for a plain vanilla desktop. . . . Jobs later admitted
he had overdesigned and overpriced the Cube, just as he had the
NeXT computer. (pp. 445–46)

These examples illustrate a couple of general facts about
Steve Jobs and the market. First, all of Jobs's products show
attention to detail and a tight marriage of design and technical function. This was certainly true of both the NeXT computers and the G4 Cube, and it was true even of the Apple
II, his first all-in design and manufacturing product. This is
why we might say that Jobs never produced a bad or low-
quality product.

But, second, quality alone in this narrow sense does not
guarantee market success. Products sell well when they offer
a large number of buyers a value. It's not enough for value that
a product be of good quality or highly functional: cost, conven-
ience, and utility are at least as important. Today, fantastically
fast and powerful supercomputers are sold to the few organizations that can pay the millions they cost. But supercomputers are not a value to everyone else due to their inconvenience
and cost. Similarly, the G4 Cube cost too much for the consumer market and it was too ostentatious for professionals.
The NeXT machines were highly advanced, but they cost too
much compared to other workstations and, as part of a closed
software environment, they didn't offer buyers enough flexi-
bility. Similarly, Jobs was furious at then-CEO John Sculley
for setting the original Macintosh's price at $2,495 rather than
Jobs's preferred price point of $1,995 (p. 170).

So it's a mistake to speak of quality apart from utility. An
excellent tool is one well-fitted to the uses to which it will be
put. Jobs recognized the truth of this principle himself: success
in the market was a way of checking that he had succeeded in
making products that were well-fitted to their use. And this
applies to entertainments and artworks as well: the Pixar
movies, for instance, were famed for their union of the best
computer animation techniques with excellent story-telling
and characterization. They were a good entertainment value.

The Individual in the Market

Most Americans who lived in the 1975–2012 period can recall being personally touched by a Steve Jobs product. For my part, though no Apple fan-boy, I learned to program on an Apple II, felt the new life that Pixar films such as *Toy Story* and *The Incredibles* breathed into animated movies, and today use an iPad. A successful product is successful individual by individual, and we all can recall moments when we were touched by great products.

Though Marxist critics have decried the market as alienating, we can see in considering Jobs's impact how each of us chose to be connected to Jobs's achievements, albeit in our many different ways at different times.

A market is a social institution founded in rights to private property, in which individuals engage in trade. And trade is voluntary exchange to mutual benefit. Thus to be able to sell in the market you must find willing buyers for your products.

Success in the market arises from the *revealed preference* of the customers. Behind each sale is a real person who decided that the product in question was worth its price, in a real-life decision with real consequences.

Compare the buyer with the critic. A critic assesses and judges a product (be it a tool or artwork, or, like most Jobs products, a bit of both). The critic may try out a product, as product reviewers do for magazines and newspapers. The critic is supposed to be knowledgeable, where a normal customer need not be. But the critic does not commit his own resources to the purchase decision. And the critic doesn't fully integrate the product into his own life and purposes. Rather, the critic's use of the product is simply a means to fulfilling his job responsibilities and what the critic says about it is, in the end, for conversation, whereas the real buyer lives with his purchases.

Thus the market does offer the final affirmation of a product. Sales of the product show that people find the product useful and attractive: that it works for them, in their lives,

to further their achievement of their goals and the fulfillment of their needs.

I remember the first iPhone I saw: the friend who was
showing it to me was in awe of its features and simple
beauty. The importance of the product was not how it met
his sense of critical acumen, but how well it served him and
what neat features it had that would give him pleasure and
improve his life.

Jobs versus Market Research

Steve Jobs was renowned for not doing market research. He
despised other corporations' obsessions with surveys and
focus groups. "Customers don't know what they want until
we've shown them," is a typical Jobs statement on this issue
(p. 143). At the launch of the Mac, Jobs asked: "Did Alexander Graham Bell do any market research before he invented
the telephone?" (p. 170). He viewed his own role to be serving as a visionary, reaching beyond the context of knowledge
that normal consumers have and projecting something genuinely new.

Jobs's approach was made possible by the fact that, as a
person with a reasonable understanding of current culture
and products, who was not wildly idiosyncratic, he could
judge whether products were good and needed based on how
well he thought they would serve his own life. For instance,
the idea for the iPod came about because Jobs was a
recorded-music aficionado. Around the year 2000, he realized
that the digital music players available "truly sucked" (pp.
383–84). Jobs and his team were better than any focus group:
they could think about how products worked in their own
lives, and that evidence was sufficient to judge if many people would find the products useful. But Jobs and his team
were also inventors who could envision new products and
their uses.

As an inventor, Jobs sought to create previously unknown
products with excellent quality and utility. He was looking
for novel features or structures that would make his prod-

ucts superior to any competitor: features such as the graphical-user interface of the first Macintosh, or the broad selection of digital music in the iTunes store, or the intuitive touch-screen of the iPod Touch and the iPhone. In computer operating systems and in smart phones, to this day the world-wide standard style and design follows in Jobs's footsteps. The Windows and Android operating systems, for instance, though they aren't Apple products, owe an intellectual debt to Jobs. Non-Apple smart phones before iPhone used many designs. After iPhone, they mostly looked like an iPhone.

A focus group can't give us the kind of test that actual sales in the market provide. When a product is sold for practical use, only then do the buyers put in the effort needed to explore its capabilities, understand them, and adapt their practices to the new. And in fact, as Jessica Vascellaro has explained, the only market research that Apple normally conducted was to gather data on their customers' traits and on how their customers use Apple products.

The limits of focus groups derive from the differences between ordinary people and inventors. Ordinary people can understand issues in a general way in the abstract, but that is no match for wrestling with their full detail in the concrete. When, as in a focus group, we are asked to imagine a new product and envision how we might use it, we're unlikely to be able to do more than relate it to the products we already know, reasoning by analogy. And the products we imagine we want now are conditioned by the environment we normally experience: unless we are tech mavens, we are unlikely to be able to see what the possibilities are. Jobs could see, and that's why he had no use for focus groups.

We didn't know we wanted these things until Jobs showed us. And once he'd shown us, we took them for granted as features of our world, just as we take Bell's telephone for granted. Innovators can't ask us what the great new future products will be: we aren't the technological visionaries. They have to show us.

Market Success and Universal Values

One influential approach to ethics was captured in the famous words of David Hume:

> We speak not strictly and philosophically when we speak of the combat of passion and of reason. Reason is, and ought only to be the slave of the passions, and can never pretend to any other office than to serve and obey them. (*Treatise of Human Nature*, p. 415)

So, according to Hume, we can only choose to act based on our desires. A recent discussion along similar lines is by Richard Fumerton. The same view is accepted in the theory of economics, which holds that people act based on their preferences or desires.

But there's a problem with this view, because it's impossible to identify basic desires that people can't go against. People die on hunger strikes and other fasts. There are suiciders and suicide-bombers. Steve Jobs himself was a vegan fanatic who often subsisted on nothing more than juice. What basic desire drives both that kind of asceticism and the indulgence of the glutton? People act against pride, too, or struggle against humility. They act for fame, or sometimes reject fame completely. In all these cases, while it's no doubt true that every person has desires, it doesn't seem to be the case that some set of basic desires explain all these differences.

And, if there are no basic, undeniable desires, the desire-satisfaction theory has the character of a self-fulfilling prophecy, since it takes the motivating desire to be whatever reasons or feelings contributed to one's choice to act in a certain way. Thus when people act against what they understand to be their own desires (as when they act self-sacrificially because they think they have a duty to do so, for instance, or when they overcome a deep-set fear) the desire theorist must assume that even so, they were driven by their desires.

Instead, it's more fruitful to view human beings as having a common set of (broadly understood) needs and capacities.

This approach has been developed by philosophers like Ayn Rand and Philippa Foot. Insofar as we seek to live and be happy, we must fulfill those needs. These basic needs include needs for food, shelter, health, knowledge, inspiration, self-esteem, and so on. Without the fulfillment of these needs it isn't possible to live long or achieve much happiness. The end-goods we buy or create, such as homes, clothing, cuisine, artworks, schools, and more, serve to satisfy these more basic needs. Similarly, the other values we pursue, such as friendship, success, and love, do the same.

And insofar as we act to satisfy our needs, we can only do so using the capacities we have. We cannot fly by flapping our arms: that's a physical capacity birds and bats have, but humans don't. To fly, we must use our minds and our hands to build tools and machines: gliders and airplanes. So human civilizations are broadly similar: what works for humans in one place (urban living, for instance, and private property) works well for humans elsewhere, too, if adapted to local culture and environmental circumstances. This is because we all have the same basic needs and capacities.

Market success, then, will by and large be a result of fulfilling real, objective needs, not arbitrary whims. Market success will derive from individual customers' decisions that the product is of value to them in the context of their own needs and their own pursuits of happiness. Because those needs, and the means that conduce to happiness, derive from the needs of the human organism as such, many individuals will have similar needs, even allowing for variation in individuals as regards taste, interests, knowledge, and wealth.

Market success is not itself proof that a product is good. Many mediocre, over-priced, or even harmful products have achieved market success. In the immediate sense, it's true that people have desires. Products that fulfill those desires can sell well. But in the longer run, it's those products that address people's real needs that we should expect to tend to dominate, if people choose products based on what actually contributes to their well-being. People don't always choose to act for their well-being, which is a big reason that harmful products can sometimes succeed. But people mostly do tend to act the sake of for health and happiness. And that's why products designed for objective human needs, like the products whose creation and marketing Jobs oversaw, could be expected to succeed.

Jobs's biographer Walter Isaacson remarks that the team at Apple that built the iPhone started the project due to their dissatisfaction with their own cell phones. "Jobs and his team became excited about the prospect of building a phone that they would want to use" (p. 456). They were frustrated with technical aspects of most of the phones available: their clunky, ugly interfaces, their difficulty of use for storing contact information or instant messaging, and their failure to be everything a hand-held computer could be. But insofar as what the Apple team sought was a phone that would do more of everything useful and be better than existing phones, they were thinking of a product that would be useful to themselves, as modern humans.

Market success was the affirmation of Jobs's success in building an efficient, effective, product. When honest, productive people chose to purchase his products or see his films, they showed that he had, indeed, created products that were valuable to people as such. It confirmed that the products were priced right (which means, having the right costs), that their quality was good, and they worked. The times Jobs failed to achieve this, he realized that he had over-indulged his love of technology and fine design, at the expense of cost-efficiency and usefulness.

When Steve Jobs did achieve market success, underlain as it was by the revolutionary character and deep design integrity of his products, it was evidence that he had achieved his goal. And his innovation and excellence touched every one of the customers who chose to buy and use the products. Thus Jobs's market success is quite properly a core reason why he is admired.

III

The Rebel

9
Marley and Steve

Jason Walker

Steve Jobs was dead to begin with. There's no doubt whatsoever about that. The register of his burial was signed by the clerk, the undertaker, and the chief mourner.

However, unlike Jacob Marley, Jobs had more than one mourner. His untimely death in 2011 brought out remembrances and accolades that may have been expected for a Nobel Peace Prize winner, but were strikingly rare for a corporate tycoon and billionaire. Jobs was praised as a visionary who improved the quality of lives worldwide. Yet one fact about Jobs, and the way that he ran Apple Computer, Inc., was hardly mentioned at that time, though it has occasionally attracted critical comment: in striking contrast to his friendly rival, Bill Gates, Jobs gave relatively little to charitable causes.

In the early twenty-first century, large corporations are expected, as a matter of course, to feature charitable giving as one essential item in their budget. And even more, upon obtaining billionaire status, corporate tycoons are expected to have pet charities. Jobs did not, and Apple abandoned efforts at charity in 1997, when Jobs resumed leadership of the company, largely as a cost-cutting measure. In further contrast with Gates, Jobs did not sign on to Warren Buffett's "Giving Pledge," in which billionaires promise to devote at least half of their wealth to charitable giving.

As Daniel Dilger reported, the perception that Jobs and Apple abandoned all charitable endeavors is mistaken. Jobs did approve Apple's participation in Bono's "Product RED" program, in which "Red" branded versions of various products would have a percentage of their profits donated toward various charities. And it was reported shortly after Jobs's death that he had been involved in a joint effort, with several other tech firms, to build a new two-billion-dollar hospital for the Stanford Medical Center.

Still, Jobs was somewhat averse to philanthropic spending, and did allocate far less of his income to charity than most of his fellow billionaires. So was the much-beloved Jobs truly worthy of his posthumous accolades, when, with respect to charity, he more resembled Jacob Marley and Ebenezer Scrooge than he did the much-less-beloved Bill Gates?

Obliged to Give?

Moral philosophers will offer very different answers to this question. For many, charity represents a moral good they call "supererogatory." Supererogatory acts or virtues are those which are to be morally praised for having been performed, but their absence is not morally blameworthy. For example, you might be morally praised for saving a kitten from a tree, but not morally blamed for not doing so. A supererogatory act like charity is often thought to be acting beyond the call of duty.

Others have argued that we have stronger obligations, that charity isn't only morally praiseworthy, but that it is a duty in itself. Peter Singer famously offers the thought experiment of a small child drowning in a fountain. If you walk by the drowning child, and refuse to stop and help, so that you can be on time for an appointment and avoid getting your new clothes wet, you would have to be truly monstrous. Failing to provide aid, in this case, would be morally blameworthy. This implies that there are cases in which a failure to help can be morally similar to the active committing of a harm. And thus, charity aimed at saving lives could be understood as obligatory, part of the moral minimum, and therefore not merely supererogatory.

Is Jobs a hero for his innovations and achievements, guilty of no more than failing to do something not morally obligatory in the first place? Or, if the failure to contribute to charity is morally blameworthy, is the American public's hero-worship for Jobs misplaced, or even perverse? *Assuming* what Jobs's critics have alleged is true, that despite his wealth, Jobs neglected the pursuit of charitable efforts, would *this* fact prevent Steve Jobs from being appropriately regarded as a morally exemplary individual, or would it mean he was guilty of a grievous moral failing?

Three Approaches to Ethics

Approaches to ethics in the western tradition can be broken down into three basic frameworks. First, there are the happiness-based ethics of Utilitarianism, most prominently articulated by Jeremy Bentham and John Stuart Mill. Under this approach, the good is defined with reference to that which best promotes the "greatest happiness for the greatest number of people." There are different ways of understanding what this means in practice: for example, Bentham emphasizes pleasure, whatever its source, whereas Mill emphasizes happiness, distinguishing the "higher pleasures" of even a dissatisfied Socrates as superior to the physical pleasures of satisfied pigs.

Mill further takes utilitarianism to be best understood as applied to *general rules*, whereas Bentham applies his utilitarianism as a means of evaluating the morality of *particular acts*. Nevertheless, the important point upon which all utilitarians agree is that moral judgments must be made based on actual results. Outcomes of human action provide the basis for evaluating the morality of that action; those promoting the most net happiness or pleasure are best, those resulting in the most pain or misery are worst.

In contrast, duty-based ethics, particularly those most associated with the eighteenth-century German philosopher

Immanuel Kant, eschews judgments about outcomes for the question of motivation. The only unconditionally good thing, Kant proposes, is a good will. By "good will," Kant doesn't mean mere benevolence or good intentions, but rather a motivation tied up in the pursuit of, and obedience to, the moral law for its own sake. Two people may, of course, perform the same action, with the same results, but we would likely judge them differently if one acted for illicit motives and the other merely because it was her belief that it was the morally correct thing to do.

Kant's ethics thus prominently turns to duty as the basis of all moral judgment, distinguished as between primary (perfect) duties and secondary (imperfect) duties. As the names imply, the former are more pressing when in conflict. Imperfect duties provide the moral agent with some legroom to apply according to circumstances, but it would be a mistake to confuse these with supererogatory moral goods. Imperfect duties are still duties.

Finally, virtue-based ethics may have a claim to be the oldest of these approaches, as this approach counts Aristotle as its founder, but their revival among philosophers in the Western tradition is merely a few decades old. Here, the idea is that we should look at character as the basis of moral judgment. Virtues are a kind of moral habit, traits of character that persist over time and through adversity, and for that matter, often most acutely observed during moments of adversity. After all, it is not just one single act that determines whether a person is morally good, or the fact that someone happens by chance to maximize happiness through otherwise trivial behavior, but rather how people live their lives as a whole that determine whether we ought, for example, to trust or befriend a person.

So how should we understand charity, as a moral act or habit, under these three approaches? In reverse order, I'll start with virtue ethics. There might at first be a question about whether the notion of supererogatory moral goods can exist in virtue ethics—particularly as virtue ethicists often accept the notion of the Golden Mean: that the right path is the middle between two extremes. A virtuous life is one of balance, not one where listed duties are checked off, with supererogatory goods merely being those things attended to after all the basics are satisfied. Indeed, if we think of supererogatory actions as those which go beyond the call of duty, it seems that the idea may be more fit for a Kantian ethic than for a virtue account.

However, Aristotle assigns an important role to judgment. Judgment is necessary because the contexts in which moral decisions are made can be very different from each other, and because sound decision-making often requires practical knowledge about your own unique dispositions or tendencies. Virtuous people may, owing to these differences, strike slightly different balances, emphasizing those strengths of character where they can more easily excel. So something like supererogatory moral goods may be possible here, if we think of them as extraordinarily virtuous acts (or better still, character traits) for individuals within specific contextual constraints.

Consider courage. If an agent generally behaves with moral distinction, but shies away from situations of danger, she might be said to lack courage. She may not be a coward, necessarily; she simply never behaves in any way that would suggest extraordinary bravery. (For example, she might be brave with respect to her career choices, but be the sort of person who would never dive into a river to save a puppy from drowning, even if the danger was minimal.) While acting with a fully expressed courage would be morally praiseworthy, failing to display it wouldn't necessarily make her blameworthy either, particularly if she developed other virtues in its place to achieve something closer to a holistic balance.

Charity, for many virtue theorists, may be like this. Aiding in the charitable efforts toward the less fortunate would be praiseworthy as an instance of the virtue of benevolence, but failing to do so would likewise not make that person guilty of any blameworthy moral infraction. At the very least, moral judgments of individuals are based on their characters taken holistically. It might not exactly be to your credit that you exerted no great effort for charity, but this may be negligible as failings go if your overall character displayed great virtue in other areas, particularly if you demonstrated the virtue of generosity in some respects other than aid to non-profit organizations.

The duty-based ethics of Immanuel Kant, however, paints a different picture. Under this framework, we are to apply a test he calls the "Categorical Imperative," a decision procedure of sorts that might very roughly be compared to the Golden Rule—the rule that you should behave toward others the way you would like them to behave toward you. Here we ask the question, would failing to provide charity to someone who needed it be even conceivable if this were the known rule, followed by everyone? Kant's answer is that it is, of course, perfectly conceivable for a world to lack anyone who displayed charity. However, he claims that it is, in a sense, a world we could not "will," at least not universally. For if we were to be, ourselves, facing destitution, and our only salvation was from the charitable act of another, we would not want the charity-avoidance rule followed. (Unless, that is, we were suicidal, but Kant has a separate argument as to why suicide would be in the highest class of immoral acts.) Because the failure here is not one of logical possibility, but rather of will, Kant concludes that charity is an imperfect duty. It thus provides a basis for moral motivation, one we are all obligated to heed, but one that can be conditioned or limited based on other potentially morally relevant factors. For example, we need not donate to every panhandler we encounter, as long as we find some way of contributing charitably to the needs of others.

Utilitarians differ among themselves, and here it's worth considering the divergent approaches favored by John Stuart Mill and Peter Singer. Mill looks to the satisfaction of higher pleasures, usually intellectual in nature, over merely physical pleasure. And as a utilitarian, he certainly believes that our actions ought in some way to contribute to the well-being of others. Nevertheless, as a philosopher influenced both by the liberal tradition and the early nineteenth-century romantics, he also favors individual "experiments in living," in which people are to be encouraged to pursue their own understandings of the good life. The limitation here is a principle that can be understood politically as well as morally: the Harm Principle. We should be free to pursue our own notion of the good, provided that we don't harm other people in the process. The Harm Principle, thus, for Mill, may provide the moral minimum for his ethics. If this is right, then failing to provide charity cannot be seen as morally blameworthy, for it represents only a failure to provide aid, not an active commission of harm.

Peter Singer, however, disagrees. His argument is simple. Consider again the analogy to the drowning child (discussed by Singer in "Famine, Affluence, and Morality"). Singer observes that few would disagree with the basic principle that, as long as providing aid, in such cases, sacrifices no morally comparable goods (or even any morally significant goods), we ought to provide aid. In this case, few would argue that the value of clean, new clothes and shoes is a moral good comparable to the life of a child. So, we morally ought to provide aid.

However, in case we might assume that we must intervene only in cases where children are at risk of drowning in front of us and we're able to save them with little risk to ourselves, Singer argues that mere distance should not be a morally relevant factor. If we know that someone is dying half a world away, this doesn't make that person's life morally less important than a person close by, certainly not in an age of instant communications and charitable organizations who specialize in providing aid to people dying of starvation and preventable diseases in these faraway places. Are their lives worth less than a pair of designer shoes, or a night at the movies?

From this, Singer concludes that choosing to purchase luxuries, beyond the bare minimum necessary to keep us productive, is morally decadent. The failure to provide charity, especially in the case of a billionaire like Steve Jobs, can only be regarded as a moral crime of the highest order.

So with this variety of perspectives established, let's turn to the case of Mr. Jobs. Without resolving the question of which moral approach is the correct one, we can see what each of them has to say about the behavior of Steve Jobs. We'll see that Steve Jobs's lack of charitable giving is not morally blameworthy. Although it could be argued that Jobs was guilty of missing some opportunities for beneficence, this, in itself, does not make him immoral, and does not detract from other virtues he displayed throughout his life.

The Three Approaches Applied to Steve Jobs

In Steve Jobs we find that a man has devoted his life to his career, earning the admiration of millions of satisfied users of Apple products. His hard work did not go unrewarded, as at the time of his death, he was a billionaire many times over. However, both in his professional life, as the CEO of Apple, and in his personal life, he devoted relatively little to charitable causes, certainly not on the order that his counterpart at Microsoft has. Is he morally blameworthy for failing to be charitable?

It seems that under Aristotle's virtue-based account, Jobs can still be regarded as a virtuous man. Had Jobs devoted more to charity, he might be morally praised for that. But this is only one of many ways that we can demonstrate morally exemplary virtues. Certainly Jobs's practical wisdom, work ethic, and intellectual accomplishments would count as morally praiseworthy too on a modern account of the virtues. (These don't make major appearances in Aristotle's *Nicomachean Ethics*, in part because Aristotle had the educated sons of the aristocracy of Athens in mind as an audience. Productiveness, as a virtue, was something that might be good for a slave, but not for an aristocrat.) There is, in Aristotle, a virtue of "open-handedness," standing as a golden mean between miserliness and profligacy, but this refers to a willingness to spend in general, not specifically for charity. As a person of immense wealth, Jobs had the opportunity to develop the virtue of "magnificence," demonstrated in ancient Greece by spending for great public works projects, but Aristotle seems to have blameworthiness in mind for people who attend to that obligation in either a shabby or vulgar way, not for one pursuing other virtues.

Under the utilitarian account of John Stuart Mill, Steve Jobs is likewise in the clear. It could be argued that by failing to attend to charity, he missed opportunities to improve the greater good for the greatest possible number of people. But certainly through his career, Jobs produced innovations that accomplished that end many times over. At least with his professional life, Steve Jobs didn't violate the Harm Principle. Jobs's status as a man who provided profound net benefits to humanity would be more than morally sufficient.

There are two possible exceptions. Jobs had a reputation for being a very difficult boss to work for, so former employees may take exception to the claim that he never harmed them. An even more compelling case could be made for his first daughter, for whom he originally refused to take responsibility. This failure certainly counts as a harm if anything does, though apparently he did put it right later.

However, the moral outlook becomes more dire for Jobs if we consider the utilitarianism of Peter Singer. Singer's argument requires that all persons living an affluent lifestyle donate to charity to the point of marginal utility, that is, until the point at which benefits decrease because we give too much money or time, reducing the net benefits we are capable of producing for others. In other words, Singer takes the view that living at any level of relative affluence while people who could be saved starve to death is immoral. Whatever personal luxuries Jobs's billions could have purchased for him, they could never be as morally significant as the lives of starving children in the developing world.

Even Bill Gates, for all the billions he has donated to AIDS treatment and various development projects, falls short of basic moral decency, according to Singer's standard. Gates, like Jobs, has enjoyed the lifestyle of a billionaire rather than prioritizing the feeding of starving people. For

Singer, personal luxuries and the products of affluence are not of moral significance, and even if they were, they are not of a moral importance comparable to the importance of saving lives.

But whereas Gates at least made an effort, Jobs did no such thing. Indeed, he might be regarded as especially morally bankrupt, in that his work was dedicated to producing luxury goods like iPhones and iPads, and making them aesthetically attractive in ways to incentivize people to spend their surplus funds on such gadgets, rather than on charitable goods. Considering how far a donation of $400 could go toward saving the lives of children, what kind of monster must Jobs have been to persuade people to spend their money on toys and gadgets, instead of saving countless lives? How could such devices be of moral value at all, much less of comparable moral value with those lives?

It turns out that Kant may have an answer to this question, though he may also have some criticisms of Jobs. With Kant, there would be a question of why Jobs acted in the ways that he did. Did he act from a sense of moral duty when he created his innovations? Or did his work solely serve the end of making him wealthier? These need not be conflicting motives, but there would be a question of which was decisive, as only an action done from a moral duty can achieve moral import, and thereby be counted as a moral action.

Even if Jobs never lied, cheated, or stole, and generally acted consistently with the moral law, this may not be good enough to regard him as morally good, if his motives were a product of something other than his sense of duty to a good will, such as mere inclination or something more illicit. So a full Kantian treatment of Jobs would involve some questions of his internal psychology. However, Kantian notions of moral value may offer Jobs a saving grace against Singer's argument.

Let's consider here Singer's premise regarding potential sacrifices of things of moral significance. Singer phrases the claim this way: "If it is in our power to prevent something bad from happening, without thereby sacrificing anything of comparable moral importance, then we ought, morally, to do it" (p. 231). Singer even suggests that a weaker version of this premise would still work for his argument, so we could substitute "anything of moral importance" for "anything of comparable moral importance."

Either way, however, Kant could suggest something that would be of moral importance, if not comparable moral importance: the individual agent as an end-in-himself. Kant holds that we must treat all individuals not merely as means to the ends of others, but also always as ends-in-themselves. This rule includes how a person treats himself, which is part of the reason why Kant argues that suicide is immoral. If the individual is a moral end in himself, then he has to count at least as much as a deserving moral end as the individuals that Singer would wish to help. Kant would argue that Singer's conclusion, that affluent individuals who attend to those things which make them happy rather than provide their entire surplus to the point of marginal utility, are acting immorally, does not follow from Singer's own assumptions. For following Singer's demands would, indeed, sacrifice something of moral importance: the individual as an end-in-himself. From Kant's point of view, Singer treats all individuals who are not "suffering" and dying from "lack of food, shelter and medical care" as mere means to the ends of those who are.

Of course, Kant does insist that assistance to the poor and needy is an imperfect duty. But self-care—attending to your own happiness—is likewise also an imperfect duty. Attending to the former at the expense of the latter would thus be, at best, morally imbalanced. We, as moral agents, are expected to use sound moral judgment to determine the best ways that we can strike this balance, and as long as we attend to these duties as such, rather than merely as products of our inclinations, then we can be morally in the clear. Naturally, this still means that Jobs may be guilty of the opposite kind of imbalance, of attending to self-care and his own happiness, while neglecting the imperfect duty to assist people in need. So while Kant certainly doesn't regard charity merely as supererogatory, and one could be blameworthy for having failed to live up to that duty, this does seem to result in a far milder assessment of Steve Jobs's moral character than he'd receive from Singer.

Doing More Good

Charity, as a supererogatory moral good, seems defensible at least on two of these accounts, Mill's and Aristotle's. Only under Kant do we find grounds for arguing that Jobs may be guilty of a serious moral flaw by failing to engage in charity in a serious way, though Kant also provides a basis to argue against the more radical conclusions of Peter Singer. But independent of whether charity should be regarded as morally obligatory or merely supererogatory for businesspeople as successful as Jobs, one other possibility should be considered. According to Elizabeth Stuart, friends of Jobs reported that he "felt he could do more good expanding Apple than giving money to charity."

What kind of good could this entail? One suggestion implied here is that benevolence need not necessarily take the form of direct payments to charitable organizations or individuals in need. When we consider people who might be regarded as benefactors of humanity over the last century or two, we might come up with a list that would include people such as Thomas Edison, Albert Einstein, Norman Borlaug, Henry Ford, Marie Curie, and Louis Pasteur, among others. As scientists and entrepreneurs, it seems that in most cases, the ways in which people contributed to humanity, the way in which they "did good," was not through donating large sums of their earnings to charitable causes. Many of these individuals may have also done that, but they are remembered and celebrated for their accomplishments in scientific research and in innovations that improved the lives of people as consumers.

We sometimes lack sufficient perspective to recognize the value of such accomplishments until many years later. Although the temptation here might be to write off Jobs's remark about "doing more good" by focusing on his work with

Apple rather than with charitable pursuits as a post-hoc rationalization, it's worth remembering that even in the pursuit of aesthetic pleasures, personal excellence, scientific curiosity, and yes, even in just making more profits by building a better mousetrap, you also benefit humanity. After all, whatever else he did, Jobs created products that brought joy to his customers, and innovated in areas of personal technology that improved the lives of countless millions. Customers, far from feeling exploited, were often happy to pay a premium for them and spend hours in line to get their hands on the latest releases. Through his career, Jobs could thus be said to have a "value-added" kind of life *vis-à-vis* the rest of humanity. Being a benefactor in this way may not satisfy the moral standards of all ethicists, as we have seen, but it nonetheless may be at least as robust a means of "doing good" as charity, if we consider real world cases of such benefits. In that spirit, I suggest that the accolades received by Steve Jobs for his innovations and creativity upon his passing are well deserved, regardless of whether he remembered to set money aside for charity.[1]

---

[1] Thanks are due to feedback from Carrie-Ann Biondi, Will Thomas, and Shawn Klein, which inspired my observations about different virtuous people striking different balances. My remark about Singer viewing individuals as mere means to the end of helping others is based somewhat on an observation that I recall from a conversation with Lester Hunt. He deserves the credit for this insight, though I deserve the blame if I've misunderstood his argument.

10
The Noble Truths of Steve Jobs

Shawn E. Klein and Danielle Fundora

Steve Jobs first got interested in Buddhism and other forms of Eastern spirituality when he was an undergraduate at Reed College. Like so many college students in the early 1970s, Jobs took acid and meditated in a pseudo-spiritual search for fulfilment and enlightenment (*Steve Jobs*, p. 41). This pseudo-spirituality took root, however, and Jobs's interest in meditation and enlightenment grew more serious. He and his college friends regularly attended a local Zen center and even set up a meditation room in their attic (p. 40).

A few years later when he was working for Atari, Jobs convinced his boss first to send him to Europe on business and then from there he made his way to India to start a spiritual journey and search out enlightenment. While in India, he came across Yogananda's *Autobiography of a Yogi* and read it several times. He continued to re-read it annually (p. 51). The seven-month adventure didn't end with his enlightenment but it did have a long-lasting effect on his life and his work.

Some of Jobs's critics argue that he was not a real Buddhist. Buddhists are supposed to be calm, level-headed, and compassionate. They aren't supposed to be intense billionaire CEOs famous for temper tantrums and interpersonal cruelty. A true Buddhist, the critics claim, would be free of anxiety, supremely joyful, and always compassionate. These are not the ways Jobs is characterized by his friends and biographers. Buddhism teaches that suffering is rooted in "thirst" and that wisdom and enlightenment come from the cessation of this drive (*What the Buddha Taught*, pp. 29, 34). Can the man who ended his famous Stanford Commencement speech advising the students to "Stay Hungry. Stay Foolish" be a Buddhist? Buddhism counsels the Middle Path, avoiding the extremes of hedonism and asceticism (p. 35). Jobs, given his various obsessions with not bathing, fasting, and carrots-only diets, doesn't typically strike us as finding the moderate path between extremes.

We're not trying to justify the claim that Steve Jobs was a true Buddhist. First, such a justification is impossible and unfair: it's not our place to judge Jobs's inner commitment and devotion to these ideals. We're in no position to know what we would need to know to make such judgments so it would be unfair to try.

Second, a litmus test of the "true Buddhist" seems contrary to the heart of Buddhism. Unlike most Western views of religion, Buddhism is more about a set of practices then professed faith in specific theological claims. There are no initiation ceremonies or tests of creed: "If one understands the Buddha's teaching, and if one is convinced that his teaching is the right Path and if one tries to follow it, then one is a Buddhist" (p. 80). To be a Buddhist doesn't mean that you have achieved enlightenment. It's to be on a path, as understood and taught by Buddhism, to enlightenment. Steve Jobs might have misunderstood or misapplied what he learned about Buddhism, but he also might just have been on his path, with much ground still to travel.

Basics of Buddhism

There's no single version of Buddhism. After millennia of spreading and evolving, there are many varieties. What ties all of them together is, first, the connection to the teachings of Siddārtha Gautama, the Buddha, and second, a few central concepts shared by all variants of Buddhism. These are the Four Noble Truths, Nonself (Anatta), and meditation or mindfulness.

The Four Noble Truths

The First Noble Truth concerns the existence of suffering (dukkha). We all suffer in some way. In an effort to show that everything on Earth is suffering, students of the Buddha have argued that there are three kinds of suffering. The first kind is "the suffering of suffering" (dukkha dukkhata) (*Heart of the Buddha's Teaching*, p. 19). This kind of suffering is associated with unpleasant sensations such as physical and emotional pain. The Buddhist philosopher Thich Nhat Hanh places the pain of a toothache, losing your temper, and feeling too cold on a winter's day into this category.

The second type is "the suffering of composite things" (samskara dukkhata). In this world, things decay. Rocks, soil, and mountains erode. Plants and animals die; and food spoils. Eventually everything that is brought together will fall apart in decay which in turn causes suffering.

The third type of suffering is "the suffering associated with change" (viparinama dukkhata). All things in life are changing. Our health changes as we endure infections and viruses. Our bodies change as we grow older. The weather varies from sunshine to cloudy to snow flurries. Such change can lead us to suffering as much as it does when we catch a cold and experience the suffering of a sore throat.

It is easy to see how nearly all of earthly life can fall into one or more of these three categories and this suggests that everything is suffering. While some Buddhists try to prove that all things are suffering, Hanh suggests, instead, that the First Noble Truth requires us to "recognize and identify our specific suffering" (p. 23).

Dukkha, then, should not be understood simply as a claim that all there is to life is suffering or that Buddhism is a pessimistic view of the world. As the above categorizations show, the word has wider connotations than simply pain. It suggests "imperfection, impermanence, emptiness, insubstantiality" (*What the Buddha Taught*, p. 17). It is a reminder that one's life and this world are finite. Although this realization can be sad or discomforting, it is not a pessimistic view; it is a realistic and objective view of existence. It is also one that is potentially liberating. Steve Jobs seems to recognize this in his famous Stanford Commencement speech:

> Remembering that you are going to die is the best way I know to avoid the trap of thinking you have something to lose. You are already naked. There is no reason not to follow your heart.

The Second Noble Truth is the cause of suffering. It is, at its core, about recognizing the root cause of suffering so that we can learn to liberate ourselves from it. Once we understand the nature of our suffering, we must discover the cause. That is, what spiritual and physical "foods" are creating this suffering so that we may stop ingesting them.

The Buddha identified four sources of suffering: food, sense impressions, intention, and consciousness. While these can bring happiness to our lives, they can also lead to suffering (*Heart of the Buddha's Teaching*, p. 31). The first source, food, brings suffering when we do not eat mindfully. Hanh argues that we must learn to eat in a way that the health of our body and spirit is maintained. For example, he advises that we ought not smoke or drink as they are toxic for our bodies (p. 32).

Sense impressions, the second source, can be toxic when they lead us to crave toxic possessions and behavior. As Hanh points out, advertisements might create in us a want for toxic things, such as alcohol. Additionally, sense impressions can lead us to experience unpleasant emotions. Television and movies contain violent and sexual images that can create feelings of lust, anger, or fear (pp. 32–33).

The third source the Buddha identifies is intention. By intention, Hanh says that the Buddha meant "the desire in us to obtain whatever it is we want." While desire can lead us to some happiness, it can also be a potential obstacle to our happiness by leading to unhealthy senses of status, revenge, wealth, or fame. Rather, Hanh counsels that we ought to enjoy the wonders of life all around us: the beauties of nature or the love of family.

116

The fourth source of suffering is consciousness. When we engage in actions, thoughts, feelings, or behavior that are toxic, our consciousness can suffer from things such as fear, hatred, ignorance, or pride. Thus, we must be mindful of what our consciousness is digesting.

Once we understand the source of our suffering, the Third Noble Truth is the recognition that we can stop engaging in the suffering-causing activities and achieve peace and happiness. The claim here is that if we learn to stop the desire or drive that is the cause of suffering, then we can end the suffering. This existence liberated from suffering and the thirst that leads to suffering is what is commonly called Nirvāna (*What the Buddha Taught*, pp. 35–37). Though Nirvāna has been understood in many ways, its core idea is an existence devoid of suffering and direct awareness of ultimate truth (p. 40).

Once we accept the possibility of ending suffering, we're ready to walk the path set out in the Fourth Noble Truths: the Eightfold Path. The path is a prescription for how to remove suffering from our lives and walk a path to Enlightenment. The Eightfold Path is a "Middle Path" between the extremes of pursuing happiness via pleasure and sensation and of seeking happiness through "self-mortification in different forms of asceticism." It includes adopting the following principles to guide your actions and lead them towards the realization of an enlightened life: Right View, Right Thinking, Right Speech, Right Action, Right Livelihood, Right Diligence, Right Mindfulness, and Right Concentration.

Anatta

In addition to the Four Noble Truths, we have to understand another key component of Buddhism, the concept of Nonself (Anatta). At its core, Nonself is a metaphysical doctrine about the existence of the self. It's a rejection of the idea, common in Western philosophy, that the self is an unchanging substance. Western religions call it a soul. Western philosophers, like René Descartes in his *Meditations*, refer to it as the thinking thing.

The Buddhist view is that individuals are composed of constantly changing mental and physical aspects, known as the Five Aggregates. The Buddhist view of personal identity is similar to David Hume's: there is no single thing we can identify as the self. We are a bundle of perceptions and sensations.

One way to understand Anatta is that all things in this world are interconnected. We're composed of different elements that are in flux. As you sit reading this, different elements have both entered and left your being which in turn enter and leave other beings that surround you. For example, if you're in a good mood that mood can spread to people you talk to or engage with. Likewise, a hostile or angry mood can create a hostile or angry environment for those around you.

Because of this interconnectivity, Buddhism teaches that we ought not to think of ourselves as single, separate individuals. Rather, everything functions as one being with the ability for all parts, objects, and living beings to affect each other. Such a worldview aids in our understanding of eliminating suffering for others. If you walk the Eightfold Path, your happiness increases, which in turn increases the happiness of everyone and everything else (*Heart of the Buddha's Teaching*, pp. 133–36).

Meditation

One last essential component of Buddhism is meditation. Buddhist meditation has two aspects: *vipashyana* and *shamantha*. Vipashyana, "looking deeply" tends to be emphasized over shamantha, "stopping", as the former is a path to realization that aids in our understanding of ending suffering. However, shamantha is also important because as Hanh points out, "If we cannot stop, we cannot have insight." In order to entertain new ideas and new behaviors, we must be willing to stop our old habits and old thought-patterns.

Buddhist meditation practice is sometimes misunderstood as something that is an escape from life or an ascetic practice cut off from the rest of living. Buddhist scholar

Walpola Rahula emphasizes the idea that mindfulness in all activities of your life is essential for the Buddhist. It's important "to be aware and mindful of whatever you do, physically or verbally, during the daily routine of work in your life, private, public or professional."

Meditation or mindfulness is both inherently spiritual and profoundly practical. It develops powers of concentration and focus that are useful for everyday living and essential for understanding the true nature of reality. The focus on the present moment and action helps to reduce anxiety and stress, while also putting your past and future into proper perspective. By clearing your mind of distractions you're better able to see things as they are and to develop an attitude of observation rather than judgment. Meditation allows you to become more of a scientist, rather than a critic, of your own world and emotions. The constant self-judging that we tend to engage in is the source of much anxiety and inner strife. There's a time and place for self-evaluation, but awareness and acceptance are basic and important steps for inner peace and understanding.

Jobs and Buddhism

There are many ways that Steve Jobs seems to fall short of Buddhist ideals. Part of the Noble Eightfold Path are proscriptions against telling lies, speaking rudely or maliciously, or otherwise engaging in talk that could inspire hatred and disharmony. Many former employees and friends report instances of Jobs engaging in these dishonorable ways of acting. And seemingly contrary to the Middle Path, Jobs was often strident and unbending in his demands of both friends and employees. His infamous "reality distortion field," in which he seemed to bend people and reality to his will, also seems inconsistent with the Buddhist focus on seeking out the truth.

Nevertheless, these failings do not disqualify Jobs from being a Buddhist. Rather, they highlight the complex nature of Jobs's personality and his life-long journey towards enlightenment. In what follows, we explore some of the ways that Buddhism may have influenced Jobs.

Simplicity and Apple Aesthetics

Jobs's aesthetic style was minimalistic and simple and he frequently pointed to Japanese Zen Buddhism as his inspiration (*Steve Jobs*, p. 128). Buddhist art is often minimalistic. Take, for example, the haiku, a very short poetry form developed in Japan. These poems strip out all features but the basic experience or moment that the poet is trying to capture.

Jobs's interest in modernist architecture was surely a part of his interest in simple, minimalistic design. But we can also see Buddhism's focus on letting go of attachments as playing a role here as well. Jobs's approach was to strip away all the unnecessary features and elements of a product. The goal was to get to the essence of the product by continually removing inessential aspects and simplifying it.

Meditation and the focus on the present moment clears the mind of distractions and excess thoughts that more often than not inhibit rather than help. By removing these excess thoughts one is able to focus on the present moment and to see what it is truly important. This in part explains the minimalistic aesthetics of Zen Buddhism and of Steve Jobs. In his drive to perfect his products, he strove to remove the excess in the product. This left only the pure essence of the product.

The User Experience

Apple is best known for creating products that are easy to use. They user-friendly regardless of the users' technological background or comfort with technology. This comes out of Jobs's commitment to simplifying. We've seen that there was an aesthetic component to this simplifying, but this was also integrated with a concern about the user's experience. Jobs wanted users to be able to employ Apple products easily and to quickly find what they needed. He wanted the experience to be natural and intuitive. Isaacson reports on the development of the iPod: "If he wanted a song or a function, he should be able to get there in three clicks. And the click should be intuitive" (p. 388).

Jobs wanted users to feel naturally connected to the product. We can see how this ideal relates to Buddhism. Meditation is about awareness in the present moment. But a bad user experience takes you out of the moment. You have to think about what you're doing rather than doing it. This self-consciousness draws you out of the task you were doing or the moment you were enjoying, such as working on a writing project or listening to a song. Simple, intuitive interfaces allow you to use the product naturally and without thinking about what you have to do. Stripping away the excess and focusing on the process of how people actually use the technology allowed Apple to develop some of the most user-friendly products in the computer industry.

Art and Technology Combined

Jobs always saw Apple and his career as sitting at the intersection of the humanities and science:

> We believe that it's technology married with the humanities that yields us the result that makes our heart sing. (*Steve Jobs*, p. 527)

Jobs was critical of Microsoft and other high-tech companies for forgetting or being seemingly unconcerned with the humanities and the arts. Jobs, from a young age, was interested in technology and the humanities. He showed a deep curiosity with the technology that was being created in Silicon Valley where he lived. But unlike many of his technology peers (such as Apple co-founder Steve Wozniak and Microsoft's Bill Gates), Jobs was not only interested in computers. While at Reed College, he sat in on classes on calligraphy and began his study of Buddhism.

The Buddhist view of the mind doesn't fit neatly into traditional Western categories. Consciousness, according to Buddhism, arises out of certain conditions. That is, visual consciousness arises out of the conditions of the eye and visible forms (*What the Buddha Taught*, p. 24). Nevertheless, it does not seem correct to say that Buddhism is some kind of materialist or physicalist view. Mental consciousness arises out of ideas and thoughts—things not sensed or perceived by our sense organs (p. 21).

What we can say is that Buddhism is non-dualist. It doesn't oppose mind to matter. It doesn't privilege one or the other. Similarly, Jobs always tried to bring both the arts and technology together. He didn't see one as more important or essential than the other: they shouldn't be separated.

In this integration of the arts and technology, we can see further evidence of Buddhist influence. Too often people segregate themselves as either artsy or a science geek. As teachers, we hear students say they don't want to take science or math classes because they prefer poetry or music. Conversely, we have pre-med students who see little value in putting effort into Shakespeare's Sonnets. For Jobs, life wasn't about just art or just technology. One was not to be privileged over the other: we should strive for the Middle Path. The best products (and by extension the best life) come out of bringing these together. You can't *just* be an artist or *just* be an engineer. To be truly great you must be both—that is, you have to bring together the arts, humanities, science, and technology: "some of the best people working on the original Mac were poets and musicians on the side. . . . Great artists like Leonardo da Vinci and Michelangelo were also great at science" (*Steve Jobs*, p. 568).

We see the same middle path at Pixar—a company Jobs helped to get off the ground and achieve success. Pixar has had hit animated movie after hit animated movie. But the company's success is not primarily due to its innovative technology. It is this technology integrated with a deep sense of what makes great story-telling. A great story without the technological medium that Pixar provides wouldn't be able to be seen and enjoyed by the millions who love *Cars* or *Toy Story*. But amazing graphics and animation devoid of the art of story-telling would quickly be uninteresting and boring.

Authenticity

Jobs always trudged a path all his own. He strove to stay true to his vision—often at great personal and professional cost. His refusal to use market research and his determination instead to rely on his own sense of what would be a good product is legendary. The famous Apple marketing campaign "Think Different" was a homage to self-reliant individualists who strove to follow their own vision—a group in which Jobs no doubt included himself. It celebrated "The crazy ones. The misfits. The rebels. The troublemakers. The round pegs in the square holes. The ones who see things differently" (p. 329). Jobs seemed to embody and strive for a kind of authenticity and self-reliance that might at first seem at odds with Buddhism.

Like most philosophies, Buddhism is interested in discovering and teaching The Truth. "What is essential is seeing the thing, understanding it" (*What the Buddha Taught*, p. 6). The Buddha acknowledged that the truth is often difficult to see and harder to accept (p. 52). According to Buddhism, the Noble Eightfold Path and meditation practices are the main ways that we can come to see and accept truth. Rahula tells us that the Buddha explained the Noble Eightfold Path "in different ways and in different words to different people, according to the stage of their development and their capacity to understand and follow him" (p. 45). The path to truth and enlightenment is not a singular or absolute one. It is unique and relative to the needs and capacities of each individual.

This leads us to meditation and mindfulness. Mediation makes you more aware of the present moment and the emotions and feelings that you experience. It does so in a way that is (ideally) free from criticism or judgment. It is just a matter of acceptance of the reality of these emotions. Instead of experiencing the feeling as my feeling (my sadness), it becomes a feeling (sadness) (p. 73). This detachment frees you to better understand yourself and to see things as they are. Through consistent mindfulness you can discover the path that best fits your needs and capacities. Thus, as Joshua Guilar and Karen Neudorf tell us, Buddhism calls for a kind of authenticity and self-reliance. As a Buddhist you must be true to yourself.

But since Buddhism teaches that there is no self, in what sense is there any reason to discover who you truly are and what your capacities are? How can you be true to yourself when there is no self?

While Buddhism teaches that there is no metaphysical soul or self, it still teaches that you have to take care of yourself (*What the Buddha Taught*, p. 60). The impermanent, composite self does exist and it is part of the Four Noble Truths to recognize this. Buddhism teaches that you should live within your means. You should take care to develop your skills and talents and work diligently. Individuals ought to develop and progress both spiritually and materially—and moreover, these go together. Material progress without moral and spiritual growth is meaningless and misdirected and there can be no moral and spiritual development without economic well-being (pp. 83–84). So rather than being inconsistent with Buddhism, the authenticity and self-reliance that Jobs embodied is deeply connected to his Buddhism.

Buddhist Icon?

Steve Jobs may not have been the ideal image of a Buddhist. As we've seen, there were many ways that Jobs seemed to fall short of the teaching of Buddhism. Nevertheless, the ideas and practices of Buddhism clearly had a life-long effect on his life, his work, and his companies.

In some ways, though, Jobs might even be the best symbol for Buddhism. Buddhism is a worldview for human beings— not for perfect beings. It is a guide for all of us who, like Jobs, are complex beings driven by many passions and drives. We, like Jobs, struggle with these passions and sometimes fall short of living up to our professed ideals. What we can learn from Jobs and Buddhism is to stay true to ourselves and to keep trekking on our path. We may not ever reach Enlightenment, but part of what Buddhism teaches is that the path is what matters (p. 81).

Enlightenment may come or it may not, but stay true to the right path and you'll be living the best life you can live.

11
Two Sides of Think Different

Robert White

Here's to the crazy ones. The misfits. The rebels. The troublemakers. The round pegs in the square holes. The ones who see things differently. They're not fond of rules. And they have no respect for the status quo. You can quote them, disagree with them, glorify or vilify them. About the only thing you can't do is ignore them. Because they change things. They push the human race forward. And while some may see them as the crazy ones, we see genius. Because the people who are crazy enough to think they can change the world are the ones who do.

—Apple's 1997 Think Different commercial

Steve Jobs regarded himself as one of the crazy ones—a misfit, a rebel, a troublemaker—pushing the human race forward. The Think Different commercial reflects Jobs's assessment of his place in history.

Walter Isaacson has credited Jobs with revolutionizing six industries: personal computers, digital publishing, animated movies, music, phones, and tablet computing (*Steve Jobs*, p. xix). A person does not revolutionize an industry, let alone six of them, through the exercise of pure physical labor. These are primarily intellectual achievements. Before a new good or service can be given physical expression, it must begin life as a thought in someone's head.

The goods and services produced by Apple (the iMac, the iPod, the iPhone, the iPad, Apple TV, Apple Watch, iTunes, iCloud, and much, much more) are ideas given physical form. Though a number of individuals contributed, intellectually, to the creation of these goods and services, Jobs provided the intellectual leadership needed to bring these individuals' ideas to fruition.

The Think Different commercial honors individuals who have changed the world by turning thought into action.

- **Thomas Edison—whose inventions gave rise to three new industries: electric power, sound recording, and motion pictures**

- **Amelia Earhart—who theorized that she could fly solo across the Atlantic, and did**

- **Frank Lloyd Wright—who projected the Earth as it might be and ought to be, and gave reality to his vision through the medium of architecture**

- **Maria Callas—whose voice objectified in emotional terms her view of human existence**

Different people respond to the commercial in different ways, depending on their value judgments. Speaking personally, I find the commercial especially moving because it is one of the few occasions in today's world when *thinking* is honored.

Some critics might judge Jobs to be hubristic for placing himself in the same category as such world-historical figures. Hubris, however, consists in an overestimate of one's achievements. Jobs earned his place in this pantheon.

The Independent Mind

Though some earlier thinkers (such as Frederick Douglass) had celebrated the self-made man, Ayn Rand was the first philosopher to explicitly identify independence as a virtue. By "independence" Rand means primarily intellectual independence. For Rand, independence is "one's acceptance of the responsibility of forming one's own judgments and of living by the work of one's own mind" (*Virtue of Selfishness*, p. 28). An independent person accepts an idea because he judges it consonant with the facts of reality, not because of how he was raised or because of what other people will think. As Tara Smith explains, the facts of reality, not the opinions of others, are the independent person's compass in life, according to Rand.

Jobs demonstrated intellectual independence throughout his life. As a teenager, Jobs's parents required him to attend Sunday school. The pastor told the class that God knows everything. The following Sunday, Jobs took to class a recent *Life* magazine, with a picture on the cover of starving children in Biafra. Jobs asked, "Does God know about this?" The pastor conceded that God did know, and Jobs announced that he did not want to worship such a God (*Steve Jobs*, pp. 14–15). At the age of thirteen, Jobs had raised what in philosophy is known as the problem of evil—how can the existence of evil be reconciled with the existence of an all-knowing, all-powerful, and all-benevolent deity? Most thirteen-year-olds would not have possessed the independence needed to question the intellectual authority of a pastor. Jobs did.

When Apple went public in the early 1980s, three hundred people became millionaires (p. 103). Money enables a person to pursue his or her values. In this sense, money can buy happiness, contrary to the popular aphorism. In the case of these newly minted millionaires, however, they adapted their values to their newfound wealth. Instead of using their wealth to serve their values, they adopted the values other people expected millionaires to have. They bought multiple houses, Rolls-Royces, and in some cases even paid for their wives to have plastic surgery.

Jobs was an exception. His new wealth did not change him. He continued to live as he judged best, not as others expected him to live (p. 105). For example, Jobs's wife and children lived in a house so modest that Bill Gates, with his

66,000-square-foot mansion, could not comprehend how the entire family could live there (p. 277).

Not only did Jobs display intellectual independence, he explicitly defended it. In his Stanford University commencement address, Jobs told the graduating class:

> Don't be trapped by dogma—which is living with the results of other people's thinking. Don't let the noise of others' opinions drown out your own inner voice. (Jobs 2005)

And in an interview with *Wired* magazine:

> To do something really well, you have to get it. . . . It takes a passionate commitment to really thoroughly understand something, chew it up, not just quickly swallow it. Most people don't take the time to do that. (Quoted in Wahl, p. 31)

To have "your own inner voice," a person must think for him- or herself. To chew something up, not just quickly swallow it, is the process by which a person thinks for him- or herself.

In certain respects, the Think Different commercial honors not just *thinking*, but *independent* thinking. After all, to think differently the individuals honored in the Think Different commercial had to first think independently. Difference is not a defining characteristic of independent thought, however. As an independent person's concern is with the facts of reality, we should expect independent individuals to eventually reach the same conclusions. To think differently, in the sense of originating a new idea, however, a person must first be an independent thinker. Edison did not conceive the phonograph by imitating the thinking of past generations. He had to think differently, and to think differently in a reality-orientated manner he had to grasp the relevant facts of reality himself.

Jobs was able to revolutionize six industries because the independent thinking he cultivated in his character from an early age enabled him to think differently. Tony Fadell recalls, for example, that his team would be working on a seemingly unsolvable problem with the user interface on the iPod, when Jobs would come along and redefine the problem so it simply went away (*Steve Jobs*, p. 389). When developing the iPod Shuffle, Fadell and Jonathan Rubinstein faced the problem of how to make the screen smaller. Jobs solved the problem by doing away with the screen altogether (p. 410). This is the hallmark of genius.

Independence and Pseudo-Independence

The hallmark of an independent person, according to Rand, is that he or she treats facts of reality as absolutes. An independent person will evaluate and question human creations, such as the laws of a country, but he or she respects as absolute facts inherent in the nature of reality, such as the law of gravity (Rand 1984, pp. 23–34).

The independent person recognizes that existence has primacy over consciousness, which means that we must conform to the facts of reality, we cannot expect the facts of reality to conform to us. The intellectually independent person is independent in the sense that he or she seeks to grasp the facts of reality first-hand, not in the sense that he or she seeks "independence" from reality.

According to Rand, the type of "independent" person who seeks to *escape* reality is not genuinely independent. Ultimately, the person who refuses to grasp the facts of reality him- or herself has to rely for his or her survival on those who have taken on this responsibility (Mayhew, p. 117). In this respect, such a person is as dependent as the one who openly parrots the opinions of others. Consider, for example, a person whose "independence" consists in rejecting modern science and embracing various forms of supernaturalism, such as astrology and psychic readings. To the extent such a person is consistent, she must rely on individuals who are reality-orientated for her survival. She might sleep on an innerspring mattress. She might use an air conditioner to cool her house during summer. She likely purchases food from a supermarket and cooks it in a microwave oven. She might listen to mantra chants on her iPod. And her ability to purchase these goods and services is made possible by the individuals who created the business she works for. Alone on a desert island, such an "independent" person would not survive long.

Though Jobs demonstrated genuine intellectual independence throughout his life, in certain significant respects he simply was not reality-orientated, and therefore to that extent lacked genuine independence. One notorious example being Jobs's refusal to bathe, because he was convinced his vegetarian diet prevented body odor (*Steve Jobs*, p. 43). Unfortunately for Jobs's colleagues, he was wrong. In fact, he stank. To check this, all Jobs had to do was lift his armpits and sniff. Despite the direct evidence of his olfactory receptors, Jobs continued to deny that which was evident to his colleagues' noses. Convention states that we should bathe regularly. Though the genuinely independent person may sometimes defy convention, in this instance Jobs was doing so in a manner that failed to respect the facts of reality.

A tragic example of Jobs's lack of genuine independence was his initial response to the diagnosis of cancer. His doctors advised surgery. Jobs refused. He attempted to treat his cancer with alternative remedies such as fruit juice and the expression of negative feelings (pp. 453–54). Unfortunately, for Jobs, and for us, cancer has a specific nature. Given the nature of cancer, fruit juice and the expression of negative feelings was never going to work. All Jobs achieved was a delay in pursuing an actual treatment, thereby endangering his health and contributing to his premature death. Reality is unforgiving.

Like the genuinely independent person, the person who is pseudo-independent will also think differently, though not in the same sense. As a first-hand thinker, the genuinely independent person may end up challenging certain received wisdoms that most people take for granted, such as that the Sun and planets revolve around the Earth, or that heavier-than-air machines cannot fly. The person who is pseudo-independent is not concerned with facts, and therefore has no intellectual qualms about propounding absurdities that clash with common sense. The genuinely independent person thinks differently because his different thoughts are in accordance with the facts of reality. The pseudo-independent person thinks differently in a way that treats the facts of reality as irrelevant to his or her conclusions.

My claim that Jobs was not always reality-orientated is uncontroversial. This fact was widely recognized by Jobs's colleagues, who repeatedly referred to what they called his "reality distortion field" (explored in Chapter 1 of this book), a concept borrowed from an episode of *Star Trek*, in which aliens possess the power to create new realities through a sheer act of consciousness. This is what Rand termed the primacy of consciousness, the belief that reality is a product of consciousness, whether the consciousness of an individual, a group, or a deity. The genuinely independent person places reality first. The pseudo-independent person places his or her own consciousness first. The primacy of consciousness is implicit in the above examples. In each case, Jobs was acting on the premise that his consciousness can rewrite the facts of reality.

Jobs's colleagues were not trained in philosophy, and there is no such phenomenon as a reality distortion field (Harry Binswanger has called it a concept of imagination, like "hobbit"), so we should not be surprised to find the concept applied inconsistently. The concept was used in at least two substantially different senses. In some instances, the reality distortion field was used to describe how Jobs persuaded a person to achieve that which he or she previously thought impossible.

In such cases, "reality distortion" is a misnomer. Here, Jobs is not acting on the premise of creating his own reality. Jobs is the one with the better grasp of reality, and his colleagues are several steps behind, playing catch-up. To paraphrase a Wayne Gretzky quote Jobs liked, he was skating where the puck's going, while they were still skating where it's been (*Steve Jobs*, p. 349). When Jobs told Corning Glass

CEO Wendell Weeks that he wanted as much of their gorilla glass as they could make for the then soon-to-be-released iPhone, and that he needed it in six months, Weeks told him that this is impossible, because their plants are not set up to make such glass. Undeterred, Jobs told Weeks, "Get your mind around it. You can do it." Almost overnight, Corning converted one of their facilities to make a glass that had never been made before. The glass was delivered on schedule (pp. 471–72). This is Jobs the independent thinker at work.

In other instances, however, the concept was used when Jobs showed an insouciant disregard for relevant facts. For example, in 1985, when Jobs was CEO of NeXT, he announced that their first computer would ship in eighteen months. At the time, all the facts indicated that this commitment could not be met. And it wasn't. The computer would not ship for another two years (pp. 226, 235). In such instances, Jobs was not identifying the relevant facts and making a judgment on the basis of those facts. Rather, Jobs was making a groundless judgment and expecting reality to comply. This is an attempt to overcome the facts of reality by sheer willpower. This is the primacy of consciousness. This is pseudo-independence.

The Glitch in Think *Different*

The Think Different commercial packages together genuine independence and pseudo-independence, treating two substantially different character traits as though they constituted a single type of human action. Perhaps this should not be surprising. Given that Jobs instantiates both himself, we might expect a television commercial that reflects Jobs's self-estimate to treat the contradictory traits in his own character as though they constituted a single package.

To appreciate what's happening here, consider the Think Different commercial at two different levels. In terms of particular examples, the commercial focuses, for the most part, on individuals who are genuinely independent. But in terms of the abstract description of these individuals, the commercial focuses on characteristics common to both genuine independence and pseudo-independence. In particular, the commercial stresses that these individuals are united by the fact that they think *differently*.

In so doing, the commercial commits what Harry Binswanger terms the fallacy of false integration. A concept is analogous to a manila file folder. In the folder labeled "surgeon," for example, we file everything we know about surgeons. Similarly, in the folder labeled "murderer," we file everything we know about murderers. As these are separate folders, our knowledge about surgeons and murderers is kept conceptually distinct. Now, imagine we never formed these concepts. Instead, we formed the concept "cutter," which denotes anyone who cuts into human flesh. In the folder labeled "cutter," we would have to file all our knowledge of surgeons and knife-wielding murderers. As a result, we will take everything we learn about knife-wielding murderers and apply this knowledge to surgeons, and vice-versa. In our mind, surgeons and knife-wielding murderers are united in a single, inextricable package (Binswanger, pp. 236–38).

This is what the Think Different commercial has done with genuine independence and pseudo-independence. As we've seen, the genuinely independent person and the person who is pseudo-independent think differently, though in substantially different ways. In focusing on a non-essential characteristic common to both, the commercial treats them as though they belonged to a single folder. This means that alongside Edison, Earhart, Wright, Callas, and Jobs, who were genuinely independent, we have to file individuals who think differently in fundamentally irrational ways. I am thinking of such individuals as child killers Nathan Leopold and Richard Loeb, holocaust denier David Irving, and clan revivalist William J. Simmons.

In focusing on a non-essential fact—that these individuals thought differently—the Think Different commercial has packaged genuine independence with pseudo-independence, so that the two become inextricably linked in our minds. So doing transforms the arguments for independence as a virtue into arguments for pseudo-independence as a virtue, and the repugnant characteristics of pseudo-independence into repugnant characteristics of genuine independence.

Judging Jobs

An unintended consequence is that this package-deal under-mines our ability to accurately identify and evaluate Jobs's character. If genuine independence and pseudo-independence are conceptually distinct, Jobs is an individual of mixed character—virtuous in some respects and vicious in others. However, if we follow the lead of the Think Different commercial and treat both traits as part of a single package, then these are not two different character traits, together they constitute a *single* character trait, which means Jobs could not have had one without the other. Thus, we will come to think that Jobs had to have his negative traits in order to have his positive traits, and vice versa. Fans will cite his pos-itive traits to cleanse his negative traits, and critics will seize on his negative traits to undermine his positive traits.

To do Jobs justice we need to recognize that genuine in-dependence and pseudo-independence are distinct character traits. Consequently, Jobs should be praised—unreservedly and without qualification—for his independence, and at the same time criticized—unreservedly and without qualifica-tion—for his pseudo-independence.

Judging a person of mixed character is always a challenge. In Jobs's case, we must focus on the essential or important as-pects of his character—those traits that distinguished him from other human beings and made him the unique individual he was. Observe that many people have gone days without bathing and have resorted to quackery when faced with a ter-minal illness.

Only Jobs possessed the independence needed to revolu-tionize six industries. That's what's important about him. That's why he was able to push the human race forward. That's why he's a hero. That's why I wrote this chapter. That's why you're reading this book.

12
The Moral Perfectionist

JARED MEYER

Your time is limited, so don't waste it living someone else's life.

—STEVE JOBS (Stanford Commencement Address)

Steve Jobs was what most people would call a perfectionist. The visionary Apple CEO was famous—or maybe infamous—for his unrelenting pursuit of perfection in all he created, down to every detail.

While this side of Jobs is well-known—his perfectionism in creating products that would enhance the lives of millions of people—there is another form of perfectionism we can ask about—perfectionism in creating oneself. We can call this kind of perfectionism moral perfectionism. As a way of looking at morality, it goes back to Aristotle, with one recent development being the theory put forward by Douglas Rasmusssen and Douglas Den Uyl.

How did Jobs shape up in pursuing this kind of perfectionism?

Moral perfectionism is about what's good for humans—not good as defined by some outside command, by personal feelings, or by social consensus, but good as defined objectively by what actions lead humans to live flourishing lives.

Steve Jobs devoted his life to the intertwined tasks of improving his creations and himself. He grew in his visionary leadership throughout his career and, through personal development, was able to refine his perfectionism and use it

137

to his benefit—and to the advantage of people all around the world.

Aspects of being a technical perfectionist and being a moral perfectionist are compatible, though the two things are not the same. Just as Jobs was never satisfied after the first prototype of a new Apple product, moral perfectionism does not treat perfection as a static quality to be achieved—one's life is never simply "good enough." Instead, perfection involves constantly striving, evaluating, and, in a real sense, becoming.

Steve Jobs had many faults, just as everyone else does. His arrogance led him to cut off productive relationships when they did not fit his immediate needs, and he was often abusive and ruthless to co-workers and competitors alike. Though I'm not trying to deify Jobs, I do want to look at his many strengths—as an entrepreneur, manager, and person—in order to provide a clear picture of what it means to pursue human flourishing.

Individualistic Perfectionism

Clearly not everyone has what it takes to be a successful tech entrepreneur, but can everyone become a successful moral entrepreneur? Both types of entrepreneurship require a commitment to reason, a desire to see things through to the end, and an inner drive to create something of value. However, whereas the tech entrepreneur's success is solidly based on other people's wishes (if no one else wants to use the product the business will cease to exist), the success of the moral entrepreneur is based on the self.

While the good is objective and based on human nature, perfection is not the same for everyone, because individual characteristics, such as Jobs's tenacity, creativity, and attention to detail, determine each person's different version of the good life. What is good for one person may not be good for another, even in similar situations. What we call "human flourishing" is not simply one-size-fits-all. As Rasmussen and Den Uyl put it, the good is agent-relative, not agent-neutral. What it means for one person to flourish is different from what this means for another person.

If you want to flourish, you don't have to mimic Jobs's business successes or his defining personal characteristics. As Jobs said, "Your time is limited, so don't waste it living someone else's life." A person's life is their own. The successes of others may offer general pointers on how to live a good life, but copying other people and ignoring your own unique personality and situation won't be enough—you have to find your own individual way to flourish.

As Henry Veatch pointed out, people possess a wide array of talents, interests, and personalities that lead to an individualized sense of the good. So the flourishing life is not just one kind of life. It's not solely the life of the philosopher or the life of the tech engineer. It varies according to the individual's own specific talents, interests, and personality.

There's a wide range of lives people can live while still pursuing human flourishing. This should not be surprising since, after all, people are extremely diverse. So, when we say that what's good for humans is objectively based on human nature, this shouldn't limit how we can pursue human flourishing, more than the eighty-eight keys on a piano limit what songs can be played. Countless beautiful rhythm and melody combinations are still possible, and this holds true for human flourishing as well.

While there are certain goods that are integral to human flourishing (such as friendship, health, wisdom, or self-esteem), the ways individuals can balance these goods in accordance with their own distinctive talents, interests, and personalities are diverse.

Ethics Is Personal

The philosopher Immanuel Kant stated that his famous categorical imperative (a rule of conduct not dependent upon the achievement of any other end or purpose) was that you should, "act as if the maxim of your action were to become by your will a Universal law of Nature."

However, the central aim of ethics should not be providing impersonal by-the-book rules for everyone to follow. That would create a very detached outlook on morality, leading ethics to lose its relevance and meaning to individual humans' lives.

But, since human flourishing is something we can know and strive to achieve, it can be universalized. In other words, the possibility of knowing that some specific action or value is good for yourself is common to all people. These values provide a basis for your conduct, but they do not have to provide the basis for every person's conduct. Diverse people do, and should, have different correct responses to situations—we're all human beings, but we're also all individuals. The bottom line is that ethics is personal—it's concerned with what distinct individuals should do in specific situations.

Steve Jobs understood that living a flourishing human life does not come from following impersonal commands. At Apple and NeXT (the company he founded after being effectively fired from Apple in 1985), Jobs created a work environment that was demanding, but flexible. The creativity necessary to develop and perfect Apple products required time to get out of everyday routines. The best ideas were spurred at the water cooler, in casual conversations in the hallway, and during Jobs's favorite activity—taking long walks outdoors. The headquarters of Apple and Pixar (another company Jobs led during his Apple exile) were specifically designed to facilitate these sorts of spontaneous interactions.

Human flourishing is an endless, very personal process that requires constant work to know yourself. Even at a relatively young age, Jobs was interested in understanding himself, the world, and life's meaning. His forays led him to India to study Zen Buddhism when he was nineteen. He experimented with psychedelic drugs and took a strong interest in art forms, especially calligraphy. Jobs commonly went on strange diets consisting of limited types of fruits and vegetables since he thought that was better for his body. While some of his experiments in efforts to better understand himself and live more fully seem odd, Jobs carried and built upon what he learned for the rest of his life. The distinctive design of Apple products, and even the name of the company, was influenced by these lessons.

There is no manual to provide by-the-book steps to living the good life. Pursuing human flourishing takes amazing effort and dedication, and a heavy dose of experimentation. While not every foray into a new interest, friendship, or experience will be right for an individual, part of human flourishing is learning from these to inform future choices and better understand yourself.

The Bicycle and Rational Man

An integral aspect of pursuing human flourishing is the use of reason—more specifically, practical wisdom. Practical wisdom involves the synthesis of all the characteristics that make up a person's nexus and inform their values. It also requires the proper use of reason to order these goods and values in an individualized way. Practical wisdom is not some theoretical game philosophers play. Rather, it's concerned with real questions as they relate to particular individuals— it is practical in its application.

Interviews with Steve Jobs make it clear he understood that the defining characteristic of humans is the use of reason. Recalling one of his most influential moments, Jobs said:

> I read a study that measured the efficiency of locomotion for various species on the planet. The condor used the least energy to move a kilometer. Humans came in with a rather unimpressive showing about a third of the way down the list. . . . That didn't look so good, but then someone at *Scientific American* had the insight to test the efficiency of locomotion for a man on a bicycle and a man on a bicycle blew the condor away. (In the documentary *Memory and Imagination*)

This is why Jobs referred to the computer as "the bicycle of the mind." Humans are tool builders—we use our unique intellect to understand the world around ourselves and then mold the world's resources to create value. This limitless view of human intellect that Jobs held is what propelled the technology boom and brought about the age of computers.

Central to the success of any entrepreneur is the ability to see future possibilities, and then act to take advantage of them. The natural entrepreneur does not wait for feedback from endless focus groups, or delay realizing his or her vision until a venture capitalist buys into the business plan. What successful entrepreneurs do is see opportunities and then, often in the face of skepticism or outright opposition from others, fully devote themselves to creating what they see as valuable.

Ayn Rand, another thinker whose ideas were influenced by Aristotelian philosophy, argued that reason is central to the very maintenance of human life. She said,

> In order to sustain its life, every living species has to follow a certain course of action required by its nature. The action required to sustain human life is primarily intellectual: everything man needs has to be discovered by his mind and produced by his effort. Production is the application of reason to the problem of survival. ("The Objectivist Ethics," p. 20)

Even though man is a "rational animal" (as Aristotle said), the use of reason is not automatic. It takes work—just as living a flourishing life takes dedication, time, and effort.

Aristotle, in his *Nicomachean Ethics*, put forward his famous "doctrine of the mean," that virtue lies between two extremes. For example, the virtue of courage lies between the extreme of cowardice and the extreme of recklessness. However, Aristotle did not simply mean that every ethical virtue arises from a moral balancing act between two extremes. Instead, a better way to understand the doctrine of the mean is to see it as the process of weighing various goods in accordance with an individual's own specific talents, interests, and personality. There are many goods in life—among them friendship, health, beauty, leisure, and intellectual pursuits—and knowing which ones to pursue, and how deeply to pursue them, is the central task of practical wisdom.

For one person, artistic pursuits may compose a larger portion of his or her life. For another, honor may weigh most heavily while artistic pursuits are not absent, but not prominent. Yet another person could value justice the greatest. While all of these values are good for humans, the specific ways they are valued vary depending on individuals' unique interests, talents, experiences, and communities.

The Never-Ending Process of Perfecting

Immersing yourself in an activity that you see as valuable is one common way you can learn more about yourself and make progress towards personal flourishing.

Jobs took his work at Apple very seriously, but similar to human flourishing, creating a "perfect" product involves substantial investment of time and effort. Reminiscing on the mental and physical toll it took to create the product that resurrected Apple from the dead (the company was ninety days from bankruptcy when Jobs returned), Jobs said that developing the iMac was one of the "neatest" experiences of his life—even though it was also one of the most demanding (*Playboy* Interview). Trying times like these lead a person to learn what their values are, and this knowledge is central to living a flourishing life.

When talking about how it felt to be forced from the company he built, Jobs said that John Scully, the man who took Jobs's place at the head of Apple, "destroyed everything I'd spent ten years working for—starting with me" (*Steve Jobs: The Lost Interview*). Jobs was so enraged that he completely divested himself of all his Apple stock, even though he could have likely earned a much higher return by slowly selling his shares. These quotes and stories of Jobs's hard-earned success and later disappointment show that just because ethics is personal doesn't mean that living a flourishing life is easy.

Failure can offer chances to re-evaluate your life, your key values, and your future goals. While Steve Jobs was undoubtedly distraught after being—temporarily—pushed out of Apple's future, he made the most of his time away from the company (and the money made from selling his Apple stock). He first founded NeXT, another computer company that was focused on the education and research markets. While the computers Jobs guided the company to develop did not sell very well (they were far too expensive), the software they used paved the way for future advances in computing technology. Jobs realized this advantage and scrapped the hardware business to focus solely on software. This turned out to be a wise move as modern Mac and iOS operating systems rely on NeXT's foundations, and NeXT's object-oriented programming made it easier for developers to create new programs.

Soon after leaving Apple, Jobs also funded what became Pixar. Creating the computer-animated images that are used in Pixar's movies takes advanced computing power and applications. This technology took a long time to develop, but less than ten years after Jobs became involved, Pixar released its first movie, *Toy Story*, to widespread praise. Success after success followed (*Monsters, Inc.*, *Finding Nemo*, *Cars*, and others) and animated films were fundamentally changed because of Jobs's leadership. This movement into the entertainment industry clearly influenced Jobs's later breakthrough products such as the iPod and iTunes store.

Living a flourishing human life is a dynamic, not static, process and requires constant re-evaluation. In a similar way, successful business requires continuous re-evaluation and re-invention of the company, its processes, purpose, and products. Jobs saw the main problem with business being that when companies grow too large and successful, they begin to believe that their process was what brought about their success. For Steve Jobs, it was, and must continue to be, the innovative products that create lasting value. However, innovation does not arise though some pre-determined formula. The line, "Well that's the way we've always done it around here" was seen by Jobs as the death knell of corporations. To avoid this problem, Jobs insisted that even after Disney bought Pixar, the two continue operating separately, with distinct staff and distinct cultures.

Just as success in business requires much more than reading the latest book on management or entrepreneurship, there's no one-size-fits all handbook on how to flourish as a person. Even within the course of your life, the process used to "know yourself" changes dramatically, along with the self that is being known. People are not the same in their fifties as they were in their twenties—people who are the same have some serious growing up to do (or they missed out on a lot of fun during their youth).

The Steve Jobs of the 1970s and 1980s differed from the Steve Jobs of the 1990s and 2000s. Being exiled from the company he started changed him in drastic ways. Without losing his trademark tenacity, he developed as a manager and as a communicator of his vision.

In Steve Jobs's twelve-year absence, Apple grew into one of the lumbering corporate behemoths he warned against. Instead of an open environment that pressed employees to always "Think Different," Apple was a lost company that had stopped working to improve itself and was content to rest on the laurels (and profits) of past successes.

Thankfully, Jobs returned and brought Apple back to its roots—as an innovative company that built the best products and developed deep relationships with customers. The rest—the iPod, MacBook, iTunes, iPhone, iMac, iPad, Apple Watch—is history.

Was Jobs a Perfectionist?

Was Steve Jobs a moral perfectionist? It turns out this is the wrong question to ask. For one, the answer cannot be fully determined as Jobs was the only person who could truly know. There are no commands from on-high as to what exactly Jobs had to do to flourish, and this makes it difficult for others, especially those who did not know him on a personal level, to judge his moral state.

From the outside, it's difficult—and usually impossible—to determine whether another human is living a fully-flourishing life. Ethics is not impersonal or based on the views of others. While relationships with others are undoubtedly important, true to its name, individualistic perfectionism centers the focus of ethics on the individual.

Another reason this is the wrong question to ask is that moral perfection is never attained, period. Perfectionist approaches to ethics are continuous in nature. You can never say, "I am finally flourishing! That was a lot of hard work and thankfully now I can stop trying."

The uplifting news is that while most people will never achieve the commercial success or fame Steve Jobs did, that is far from all that matters in perfectionist ethics. What matters is that each person strives to more fully understand and live his or her life. For most of us, that does not mean we need to revolutionize four major industries (computing, telecommunications, music, and motion picture in Jobs's case). It generally means having positive relationships with friends and family, following intellectual and artistic pursuits, being in good health, pursuing leisurely hobbies, and finding enjoyment in productive work—"genrally" because the specifics and mix of these generic goods will vary quite a bit from person to person.

Steve Jobs created an unquestionably successful career for himself. His innovativeness is still being felt today—from Apple's new products to the evolving landscape of technology. He had a vision for the future of computing and, through his efforts, was able to turn his ideas into reality.

Steve Jobs's life showed that humans have the capability to remake their lives, and sometimes the world, as they desire it to be. In his words:

> When you grow up, you tend to get told that the world is the way it is and your life is just to live your life inside the world, try not to bash into the walls too much. That's a very limited life. . . . The minute that you understand that you can poke life and actually that if you push in something will pop out the other side and that you

can change it, you can mold it, that's maybe the most important thing. (*Steve Jobs: One Last Thing*)

It's in the process of realizing this vision that Steve Jobs offers a unique case study for understanding perfectionist ethics—specifically individualistic perfectionism. He shows us that living a flourishing human life is difficult, requires constant re-evaluation, and, most importantly, is unique to each individual. Moral entrepreneurship is possible and, as with market entrepreneurship, its rewards are limitless.

13
Does Apple Know Right from Wrong?

JASON IULIANO

Apple is known for a lot of good things. The iMac. The iPod. The iPhone. The iPad. Unfortunately, Apple is also known for its darker side. When the company is not improving our lives by releasing revolutionary products, it's busy engaging in activities that are sometimes less than praiseworthy. From the Foxconn suicides to child labor to environmental pollution, Apple has been involved in some morally questionable situations (see the articles by Sam Gustin, Juliette Garside, and David Barboza).

Whenever some Apple wrongdoing comes to light, people always debate whether the company is morally flawed. In light of the Foxconn suicides, *Wired* magazine even ran a cover story titled "1 Million Workers. 90 Million iPhones. 17 Suicides. Who's to Blame?" For many people, the answer is Apple itself. They believe that the corporation is at fault for the suicides. The same question could be asked with respect to Apple's child labor transgressions, its environmental pollution, and even the tax evasion charges that forced Tim Cook to testify before Congress. Who's to blame?

However, for philosophers there's an even more fundamental issue: is Apple the kind of entity that can be praised or blamed for its actions? Does it make any sense to blame Apple for anything it does? In other words, is Apple a moral agent?

Jason Iuliano

What Makes You a Moral Agent?

I hate wasps. If you've ever been stung by one, you surely hate them, too. When a wasp manages to find its way into my house and sting me, it probably makes sense for me to blame myself for not sealing off all the openings carefully enough. It may make sense for me to blame the exterminator for not finding and eliminating all the wasp nests in my yard. It might even make sense for me to blame my neighbor for borrowing my wasp and hornet killer and not returning it. There's one individual here; however, here that it doesn't make any sense to blame. That individual is the wasp.

Why is this? If anything, the wasp is the direct cause of my injury. If it hadn't stung me, I would have been able to continue on and enjoy my day. The answer lies in the wasp's lack of moral agency. The wasp is not an *agent*, in the sense of someone who purposefully acts. The wasp has no capacity to make a moral decision and therefore can't be held accountable for its actions.

So, who or what does qualify as a moral agent? Most philosophers have identified two conditions for moral agency. First, the agent must be autonomous. Second, the agent must have the capacity to distinguish between right and wrong.

The wasp passes the first hurdle (autonomy), but it clearly fails the second. I have not yet met a wasp that has pondered the morality of stinging me—if you find one, please let me know. You and I, on the other hand, meet both conditions. We control our actions, and we're able to make value judgments about such actions. Combining those two, it follows that we have the ability (even if we frequently fail) to let our value judgments influence our actions. Therefore, we are moral agents.

Despite the apparent clarity of this definition, there are a whole slew of intermediate cases. Take animals, for instance. It seems like dogs are pretty smart. They appear to debate the issues confronting them (admittedly in a simplistic manner) before taking action. Could they possibly be moral agents? To go one step further, how about chimps or apes? Animal moral agency is a hot debate in philosophy at the moment. I won't pursue it here, but it does illustrate the point that there can be different opinions about who or what is a moral agent.

Instead, let's look at another cutting-edge and contentious philosophical debate. Can corporations be moral agents? In particular, when Apple does something good like donate to charity or something bad like contract with factories that employ child labor, does it make sense to praise or blame Apple itself? What do you think? Does Apple approach the world like a pesky wasp—buzzing about based on pure instinct? Or does Apple approach the world like you and me—capable of knowing right from wrong and using that knowledge to guide its actions?

Apple's Desires

Intentionality is at the heart of the debate over corporate moral agency. Intentionality is mental directedness—the ability of minds to represent properties. Believing, desiring, fearing, loving, and hoping are all intentional states. You can pick out an intentional state by the fact that it exhibits a mental relation with some object or state of affairs.

For example, anyone who has a desire must have a desire that is directed towards some thing or some occurrence. Someone could desire a new iPad Air. I could desire popcorn to eat while I stream a show from my Apple TV. Or you could desire a new app for your iPhone. However, none of us can form a desire in isolation. Our desires must be directed towards some object or state of the world. This feature is what makes desire an intentional state.

On the other hand, flying, sailing, and talking are all non-intentional relations. They do not speak to the mental properties of the entity that is performing the action. A plane can fly. A boat can sail. SIRI can talk. As you can see, whereas intentional states give insight into the inner workings of the mind of an individual, non-intentional states do not.

Some people take the view that business corporations like Apple are true intentional agents. Corporations, just like you and me, have the capacity to form and unform desires, beliefs, wants, and other mental states and are able to do so in a rational manner. Proponents of corporate moral agency (CMA) argue that corporations like Apple are intentional agents.

To many people, it seems obvious that Apple is an intentional agent. Apple fears; it loves; it worries, and it even gets angry. It has wants, hopes, and desires that it seeks to fulfill. So we can point the finger at Apple and blame it for wrongdoing. Newspapers and magazine articles routinely make this assumption. Journalists just can't resist attributing mental states directly to the corporation.

For instance, a recent piece in the *Washington Post* pronounced, "Apple loves Clean Designs." While discussing the feud between Apple and Samsung, a PBS article stated, "Apple is upset over the Google Android phone operating system used by Samsung and other manufacturers." And a headline in *Forbes* boldly proclaimed, "Apple's New iPads Show Company Believes It's Alone in the Tablet Market."

Notably, these excerpts don't say, "Tim Cook loves clean designs," "Apple's shareholders are upset," or "Apple's board of directors believes it's alone in the tablet market." Instead, it is Apple—the corporation itself—that possesses these mental states.

We'll call this way of looking at things the theory of Corporate Moral Agency. Believers in Corporate Moral Agency seem to take claims that Apple can think or feel, love or hate, quite literally.

In response to this claim, you're probably thinking, "Not so fast! When people say things like, 'Apple wants to release a new iPhone next year,' they don't mean it in a literal sense. Instead, we should take their statements metaphorically."

Indeed, this is a common argument against the existence of corporate intentionality. As William G. Weaver has written, scholars who argue that corporations truly possess mental states have simply create "a metaphysics out of an accident of metaphor."

But it's not that straightforward. As we'll see, some serious thinkers do argue that no metaphor is involved. According to these writers, a corporation like Apple does quite literally think, feel, and make decisions. If they're right, Apple does possess Moral Agency, and can reasonably be praised or blamed for its actions.

Is Apple More than the Sum of Its Parts?

Opponents of Corporate Moral Agency don't believe that groups have mental states (see the articles by Manuel Velasquez, David Ronnegard, and R.S. Downie). They hold that the people who do think that way have been duped. To attribute mental states to a corporation is always an indirect way of attributing mental states to its members. Therefore, to say that Apple wants to produce innovative products is simply shorthand for saying that all or most of Apple's employees, or perhaps Apple's CEO or board of directors, want to produce innovative products. Many opponents of Corporate Moral Agency would agree with Anthony Quinton that an organization like Apple is nothing more than the sum of its parts.

Defenders of Corporate Moral Agency strongly disagree with this claim. In their view, groups can be divided into three distinct categories: 1. pure aggregates, 2. unorganized groups, and 3. incorporated groups—the last of which does indeed exhibit intentionality.

At the most basic level is the *pure aggregate*. This group is composed of individuals who share some common characteristic but are not co-ordinating their actions to achieve a common goal. "Shoppers at an Apple store," "people with blonde hair," or "middle-class Americans" are examples of *pure aggregates*. If someone were to say, "The shoppers at the Apple store want to donate to Apple's favorite charity Product Red," the speaker could mean only one thing: all or most of the shoppers want to donate to Product Red. Although the individuals possess intentionality (namely the desire to donate to Product Red), there is no group intentionality to speak of. Accordingly, the group cannot be a moral agent. Therefore, if someone were to follow up the first statement and say, "The shoppers at the Apple are morally praiseworthy," that person would just mean that all or a majority of the shoppers deserve moral commendation. So far the two sides in this debate are agreed.

A more complex collective is the *unorganized group*. Although the members of this group have co-ordinated their actions, the group itself lacks decision procedures. Examples of *unorganized groups* include two people who are walking together and a group of beachgoers who have banded together to save a drowning child. Members of these groups have joined together and co-ordinated their actions to achieve a common goal (walking together and saving a drowning child, respectively). However, these groups still lack internal decision-making procedures. There is no leadership structure or locus of decision-making authority that would control these groups in other circumstances. Although these groups have a central goal, their mental states are still reducible to the mental states of their individual members. Accordingly, this group also lacks intentionality. Again, both sides agree.

Finally, the third and most complex type of collective is the *incorporated group*. This is (according to one side in the debate) the only group that exhibits intentionality. Corporations are perfect examples of *incorporated groups*. They have standing decision-making procedures that allow the group, as a whole, to update its beliefs and revise its goals. Here's where the divide occurs. Whereas opponents of Corporate Moral Agency again see no evidence of group intentionality, proponents of Corporate Moral Agency believe that corporate decision-making procedures are constructed in such a way as to produce mental states that can properly be attributed to the corporation itself. According to this point of view, Apple really does have a mind of its own—a mind that's quite distinct from the minds of its employees and stockholders.

Does Apple Make Its Own Decisions?

Peter French has mounted one of the most comprehensive defenses of Corporate Moral Agency. In a number of books and articles, he argues that corporations possess Corporate Internal Decision structures that allow them to qualify as moral agents. French identifies two main parts to this Corporate Internal Decision structure: 1. an organizational hierarchy that sets forth the corporate power structure and 2. rules that indicate when a decision is validly made and can therefore be attributed to the corporation itself.

Let's suppose Apple needs to decide whether or not to pay a one-time dividend to its shareholders. In Apple, as in other corporations, the Board of Directors makes this decision. On the table before the Board members lies a daunting stack of papers that has been drafted by subordinates for the purpose of informing this decision. Some of the papers have been prepared by the Chief Financial Officer. Others have been prepared by Apple's general counsel. Yet others are recommendations from the Senior Vice President of Marketing on better ways to use the money to grow Apple's profits. All of these reports have been developed within Apple's Corporate Internal Decision structure. According to French, employees' personal reasons for wanting the corporation to act in a certain manner (either pay the dividend or withhold it) will be diluted by virtue of the fact that they have been filtered through Apple's Corporate Internal Decision structure.

For example, the General Counsel may personally want the dividend to be paid because he owns many shares of Apple and wants to receive a large payout now. However, Apple's Corporate Internal Decision structure requires him to prepare the report from an impersonal vantage point. The Corporate Internal Decision Structure—as governed by corporate law—forbids personal considerations from coming into play and works to prevent this from happening.

After reviewing and discussing the reports, the Board of Directors votes to pay out a dividend. They, too, have evaluated the information from an impersonal perspective. By voting, French maintains, the Board is ratifying a corporate decision based on corporate reasons, not aggregating a variety of personal decisions based on personal reasons.

In fact, when the Corporate Internal Decision structure is followed, the corporation has reasons for paying out the dividend that are distinct from any personal reasons individual Board members may have had. This would be true even if all of the Board members personally preferred that the dividend be withheld yet still voted to pay out the dividend. When these discrepancies arise, it is actually evidence of a well-functioning Corporate Internal Decision structure. French argues that the corporation has its own reasons for acting as it does, and therefore, its intentionality cannot simply be a mere aggregation of the preferences of its members.

The Apple iMind

Peter French is not the only one to advance a theory of corporate moral agency. Christian List and Philip Pettit have developed one of the most innovative accounts of Corporate Moral Agency. Their argument is based on the doctrine of functionalism. Functionalism is the view that mental states are defined, not by their internal characteristics, but rather, by the manner in which they function in a given system. The central idea of functionalism is that *thinking* is equivalent to *computation*; our minds are essentially computing machines. According to Paul Churchland, functionalism is currently "the most widely held theory of mind among philosophers, cognitive scientists, and artificial intelligence researchers." Therefore, its application to Corporate Moral Agency should be given careful consideration.

As a basic illustration of how functionalism works, consider the concept of desire. A functionalist would identify desire according to the causal role it plays within a system. For instance, the mental state of desire would occur when certain inputs are introduced into a system and the system reacts by producing a certain desire-related output. More specifically, desire could be identified as the mental state that results when a system experiences a stimulus that causes it to work towards achieving a goal.

Functionalism has frequently been used to defend a theory known as Strong Artificial Intelligence. According to this view, if your Mac were to run the appropriate software, it would be capable of experiencing mental states and would have a mind of its own. Can you even imagine how long the lines would be on launch day if Apple were to develop this software and release it as iMind?

Although the release of iMind is likely far off, the day of corporate minds is already here, at least according to List and Pettit. These two philosophers build off this functionalist framework to show that a corporation functions in the appropriate manner in order to be considered a moral agent. In particular, they argue that decision-making procedures allow corporations to form and unform intentional attitudes and to act on those attitudes in a rational manner. Like Peter French, List and Pettit identify a distinction between personal mental states and corporate mental states. In particular, they argue that, because of the distributed decision making that occurs in corporations, corporate mental states are almost certain to diverge from individual mental states.

According to this view, it is possible to think of Apple as a brain and to think of the members of the corporation as individual neurons. Employees have their own personal reasons for taking actions and their own mental states; however, the process by which they interact with each other subordinates these personal intentions and allows a collective corporate intention to emerge.

So far, we've seen that Apple is an autonomous agent. It has desires, beliefs, and other intentional states, distinct from the intentional states of its members. This satisfies the first condition for moral agency, but what about the second? Does Apple have the ability to evaluate whether a given action is moral?

Knowing Right from Wrong

Proponents of Corporate Moral Agency emphasize that in order for an agent to be held morally accountable, the agent need only possess the capacity to make value judgments. The agent doesn't actually need to consider the morality of a given decision—the mere potential to do so is sufficient.

There is a strong—and straightforward—argument that corporations meet this requirement. The line of thought is as follows: the individual humans who collectively make up the corporation have the ability to make value judgments in their individual capacities. Nothing prevents individuals from making value judgments in a collective manner. Therefore, the corporation, as an entity, has the ability to evaluate the morality of its actions.

Like in the case of intentionality, the corporation can reach moral conclusions that differ from the moral conclusions of any of its members. Again, this is possible because of decision-making structures within the corporation. List and Pettit develop a judgment aggregation paradox that shows how this disconnect can occur. Their example is not meant to replicate precisely the decision-making process within a corporation. Instead, it is meant to provide a basic example that can be generalized to the broader corporation.

Suppose Apple needs to choose a new processor supplier for its upcoming Apple Watch. Apple has settled on one factory but will only proceed with the deal if working with the factory is, on balance, a morally good decision. The corporation tasks three executives with determining the morality of the action. Amongst themselves, the executives decide that the decision would only be moral if the factory is 1. environmentally friendly and 2. economically beneficial to the local community. In other words, the executives agree that the decision to source Apple's processors from that factory should be affirmed only if those two conditions are met.

Executive A believes that the factory is both environmentally friendly and economically beneficial, so he votes that the deal is moral. Executive B believes that the factory is environmentally friendly but also that it would be economically harmful to the local community; accordingly, he votes that taking the deal would be immoral. Finally, Executive C feels that the factory is not environmentally friendly but that it is economically beneficial to the local community. Due to his concern over the negative effects on the environment, he believes that accepting the deal would be immoral. The votes of the executives are reproduced in the table below.

Apple's Own Moral Compass

	Environmentally Friendly?	*Economically Beneficial?*	*Moral?*
Executive A	Yes	Yes	Yes
Executive B	Yes	No	No
Executive C	No	Yes	No
Majority	**Yes**	**Yes**	**No**

From this voting pattern, we see that each premise has majority support, but the conclusion does not. More specifically, the majority belief is as follows: 1. the factory is environmentally friendly; 2. the factory is economically beneficial to the local community; and 3. it would not be moral to finalize the deal with that factory. Since the executives have already stipulated that the act would be moral if both criteria are met, this set of beliefs is inconsistent.

In circumstances like this, there are two options: the corporation can adopt either a premise-based approach or a conclusion-based approach. If the corporation goes with the conclusion-based approach, it will lack any justification for reaching that conclusion (after all, a majority of its decision makers believed that the factory was environmentally friendly and a majority believed that it would economically benefit the community). If, however, the corporation adopts a premise-based approach, it will experience no such problem.

Observing this dilemma, List and Pettit argue that corporations have no choice but to adopt the premise-based approach. Doing otherwise would preclude corporations from providing reasons for their actions. List and Pettit emphasize that, without the ability to provide reasons for their actions, corporations would be irrational and unpredictable agents. Since corporations are not irrational and unpredictable agents, they must, in practice, utilize the premise-based approach.

This insight shows that corporations such as Apple are agents, and Apple's intentional states and moral judgments are not reducible to the intentional states and moral judgments of its members. Apple has its own reasons for acting and evaluates the morality of its actions from its own perspective. Because of this, Apple is a full-fledged moral agent.

The Upshot

It's one thing to say that Apple is a moral agent. However, it's quite another thing to say why that matters. Proponents of Corporate Moral Agency (like P.A. Werhane and R.E. Freeman) argue that there is a responsibility deficit that frequently arises when groups take actions. For instance, in a tight group of cars going dangerously faster than the speed limit, each individual driver may rightly choose not to slow down for fear of causing an accident. In this scenario, no individual driver is blameworthy for speeding. After all, any driver who unilaterally slowed down would make the situation worse. Despite the absence of individual culpability, it nonetheless makes sense to say that all of the drivers were responsible for creating the dangerous situation.

When corporations take morally bad actions, individuals within a corporation can frequently disclaim responsibility for any number of reasons. Perhaps every individual was reasonably unaware that the action would cause harm; maybe each one believed that he could not mitigate the harm or that failure to go along with the group would only increase harm. By holding corporations like Apple morally accountable for their actions, we greatly reduce the responsibility deficit. Even when none of the individuals within the corporation is morally blameworthy, the corporate entity as a whole can still be the subject of moral rebuke and legal sanction.

Do you think that a company like Apple is an entity capable of acting morally or immorally, independent of the beliefs or wishes of the individual humans who work at Apple? Regardless of which side of the Corporate Moral Agency debate you ultimately come down on, this chapter may have given you some ideas about what it means to be a moral agent. And maybe the next time you come across someone asking, "Is Apple to Blame?" you'll have a different perspective on what the question really means.

IV

The Misfit

14
Close Your Eyes, Hold Your Breath, Jump In

PAUL PARDI

For the launch of the Macintosh, one of the most important product releases for Steve Jobs and Apple, the Mac team wanted to include a calculator application and a young engineer named Chris Espinosa was tasked with the work.

Jobs rejected Espinosa's first version as inferior but, in his own way, encouraged Espinoza to keep working. In subsequent design meetings Jobs would ask for a tweak here or to add pixels there but Espinosa could not seem to land a design that would please Jobs. Finally in one design review, Espinosa came in with a different kind of app. He created what he called "The Steve Jobs Roll Your Own Calculator Construction Set."

It was a tool that allowed Jobs to modify the look of the parts of the calculator to his liking. After a few minutes of playing around with the tool, Jobs got the look exactly the way he wanted it and the design Jobs came up with not only shipped with the first Macintosh but remained in subsequent versions of the operating system for fifteen years (*Steve Jobs*, p. 132).

While this anecdote supports the contention that Jobs was a control freak, it points to another characteristic that has philosophical relevance: Jobs relied heavily on intuition. He had to touch, see, and experience things in his world until he found what he couldn't describe with words. Steve Jobs tended to live his life in the moment. His world was one of discovery and he would come to know purity, truth, and even perfection, by encountering them. His life was guided by these principles—the principles of an artist—not by a master plan neatly written out in project specification and carefully supported by consensus and data. Jobs's life most closely aligned with the philosophical worldview called *existentialism*.

Existentialism

Existentialism in all its varieties is difficult to capture in simple terms partly because existentialists tend to eschew labels and, almost by definition, refuse to be defined. Existentialism describes a way of being in the world. Though it can be described philosophically, it's not a creed or a collection of propositions. It's the *act* of living and not a product of abstract thought. The label can be applied, if at all, to the story of a life lived rather than to specific words spoken or ideas held.

Existentialist philosophers tend not to write purely analytic work characterized by precise terms and logical arguments. They write narratives about man's struggle with existence and meaning and the journey or path that may provide that meaning. This focus tends to make existentialist writings either highly relatable or highly abstract. Many readers of *Fear and Trembling* by Søren Kierkegaard, the father of modern existentialism, see that book as an attempt to explain why Kierkegaard broke off his engagement to his love Regine—something that tortured him his entire life. The existentialist novelist Fyodor Dostoyevsky in his *The Brothers Karmazov*—often considered the greatest novel ever written—attempts to work out problems of ethics, religion, and epistemology in a fast-paced *narrative* told through the eyes of three brothers. Providing us with an *analysis* of these issues was not his concern.

Similarly, every detail of Jobs's work and life was part of an overall story that was the essence of how he defined his place in the world. There were no trivial details in a computer design just as there are no trivial words in a great novel. The details are not trivial because they make up the narrative of your life which, when lived with purpose, is not trivial. For an existentialist like Jobs, each atomic part of a design or the engineering of a product contributes to the meaning of the whole work and the end product is integrated into his (and hopefully his customers') life's narrative.

Jobs stated that his goal in creating Apple and its products was "to make a ding in the universe" (*Apple Revolution*, p. 43). He would be dissatisfied with anything less. His obsession with perfection—he once called a cooking knife in a French shop "ruined" because the manufacturer failed to remove a spot of glue in the handle (*Steve Jobs*, p. 344)—and "getting it right" was fueled by this goal. He would labor days and sometimes weeks over minor tweaks to a case for one of his machines. He tearfully stopped a rehearsal for the launch of the first iMac when he learned that the CD drive in the device was of the tray kind rather than the more elegant slot model (p. 351).

The authentic life is an expressive life of just the type that Steve Jobs attempted to live. He was called "mercurial" by those closest to him, something he acknowledged and even poked fun at (p. 234). If he felt angry, he might lash out at a beloved friend. If he were hurt or frustrated or elated and joyful, he would cry in front of peers, partners, and even customers. Authenticity means being as real as you know how and expressing that in word and deed, for better or worse.

Existentialists tend to live life "in the moment." They focus on attempting to turn possibility into actuality. They have a vision of what they want their life to mean and what it could be and they attempt to exercise their will to bring that vision into reality. As most of us know, this is much easier said than done. Actualizing everything we want to become is foiled by illness, financial loss, the will of others, and even our own weakness of will. This failure to fully realize our lives (become our truest self) results in what Kierkegaard captured in the term *despair*. Despair for existentialists isn't the same as the emotional state of depression (though they do, at times, go together). It's the experience of living a less than fully actualized life—of discovering a gap between the actual and the potentially real.

Many of us do not have an active knowledge of this gap but we have a sense of it. We have a longing to be more than we are, to be a better person, to leave a mark, to make a dent in the universe. We strive for it but can never seem to achieve it. This angst causes us to create facades and tell lies to ourselves and others so we hide our failure to actualize our possibilities. The greater and deeper the lies, the less authentic our lives may become. Psychologist Ernest Becker, in his great work *The Denial of Death*, was leveraging the philosophy of Kierkegaard when he described this mental defense as "character armor."

Bad Faith

The French existentialist philosopher Jean-Paul Sartre attempted to unpack this idea in a way similar to Kierkegaard. The inauthentic person is the one who lies to himself and thus creates a fiction about who he is and gets others to believe the fiction is reality. A person who constructs this persona acts in what Sartre called "bad faith." The person who acts in bad faith is not intentionally lying to others (that is, willingly telling them falsehoods). Rather, the person is actually lying to themselves and they know this. These lies create an internal conflict that makes being authentic impossible.

Sartre writes,

> To be sure, the one who practices bad faith is hiding a displeasing truth or presenting as truth a pleasing untruth. Bad faith then has in appearance the structure of falsehood. Only what changes everything is the fact that in bad faith, it is from myself that I am hiding the truth. Thus the duality of the deceiver and the deceived does not exist here.

Jobs would have none of this. If a product design, the layout of one of his stores, or the organization of one of his product groups was faulty, he'd call it "shit" and demand that it be redone (*Steve Jobs*, p. 122). Authenticity for Jobs took on a form of identity. A poorly designed product, store, process, factory, or circuit board represented a flaw in Jobs himself. True authenticity meant demanding of his creations the same excellence that he demanded of himself. To do less is inauthentic.

Steve Jobs recollected that the vital spark of "the Sixties" (really the early Seventies) was:

> that there was something beyond, sort of, what you see every day. It's the same thing that causes people to want to be poets instead of bankers. And I think that's a wonderful thing. And I think that that same spirit can be put into products, and those products can be manufactured and given to people and they can sense that spirit. (*Triumph of the Nerds*)

Jobs was famous for his "reality distortion field" which colleagues defined as his ability to talk about falsehoods as if they were true. Jobs would regularly deny the impossibility of product release dates, or misstate facts as if the falsehood were absolutely true. While this might appear to be acting in bad faith, it's really very consistent with this drive for self-actualization. As far as many could tell, Jobs actually believed the reality he was creating. He was not willfully lying to himself or others. Rather, he constructed the reality he wanted to be true. His biographer, Walter Isaacson, described it as a "complex form of dissembling" where Jobs would state something he wanted as if it were true without consideration for what actually was true (*Steve Jobs*, p. 118). This is consistent with an existentialist theme that reality itself is malleable.

Gates the Pragmatist

Jobs's sometime collaborator and more often nemesis Bill Gates was a software engineer at heart and built a company which focused on creating the greatest possible business impact. He understood the utility of software and how it could change the world. Gates's master stroke was not creating a work of technically advanced art but establishing a business arrangement with IBM that would help him grow a fledgling software company into a global leader. This arrangement focused on a piece of software that was rather boring: a rudimentary operating system that would help office workers get things done on a personal computer. It wasn't flashy, it wasn't perfect, but it was functional, saleable, and highly utilitarian.

As a computer scientist and technologist, Gates was very much at home in the world of the rationalist—a philosophy that focuses on reason as the best way to discover truth and make decisions about how we ought to live. But Gates was also skeptical of using reason alone to make decisions. In an interview with Michael Kinsley he stated:

> Rationality only goes so far. . . . There's a lot of latitude in terms of what's rational. If you feel like getting involved with that, *if it has this positive benefit*, then you'll put more time into the specific strategy that is rational to going [*sic*] after that opportunity and maybe coming up with something that in the long term is very rational. (*The Warren & Bill Show*, emphasis added).

Jobs was even more skeptical of the utility of pure reason and he and Gates were more alike than dissimilar on this point. Rather, Gates tended to part ways with Jobs by putting more value in building utilitarian products that could be commoditized and would reach the largest possible audience. For Gates, there was no "ideal" computer system or user experience that Microsoft should work to build. Instead, Gates's version of changing the world was to build Microsoft primarily *as a business* with a single, measurable, and immensely practical goal: a computer on every desktop and in every home. His post-Microsoft philanthropic work similarly focuses on utility and solving real-world problems for the most people possible ("Water, Sanitation, and Hygiene"). This focus on practicality and utility puts Gates squarely in the *pragmatist* camp.

Pragmatism is built on the foundation that talking about truth as an absolute that must be discovered is wrongheaded. For the pragmatist, the human intellect is fallible and truth is "epistemically opaque." That just means that it's not possible to have access to all the relevant facts needed to arrive with certainty at a conclusion. Even if we could, being able to understand how those facts fit together in just the right way is beyond our ken. Rather, we take what information we do have, admit it's inadequate, and attempt to create theories and a way of life that gives us the most benefit and the least costs.

One of the early Pragmatists, William James, attempted to give a general sense of how a pragmatist should approach certain theoretical problems by describing a method:

> The pragmatic method . . . is to try to interpret each notion by tracing its respective practical consequences. What difference would it practically make to anyone if this notion rather than that notion were true? If no practical difference whatever can be traced, then the alternatives mean practically the same thing, and all dispute is idle. (*Pragmatism*, p. 14)

Jobs seems to have equated a focus only on practical concerns with being no better than average. His existentialism led him to sacrifice market share for control that would, in his mind, allow him to achieve a Zen-like perfect balance in his products. More importantly, he eschewed a purely pragmatic approach because it involves too many compromises. Jobs built products for himself first and he would resist compromising on any part of a product's design if it resulted in something he would not want to use himself.

In fact Jobs channeled these ideas no more strongly than when comparing Apple's products to Microsoft's. When commenting on Microsoft's music player, the Zune, he stated:

> The older I get, the more I see how much motivations matter. The Zune was crappy because the people at Microsoft don't really love music or art the way we do. We won because we personally love

music. We made the iPod for ourselves, and when you're doing something for yourself, or your best friend or family, you're not going to cheese out. If you don't love something, you're not going to go the extra mile, work the extra weekend, challenge the status quo as much. (Isaacson, *Steve Jobs*, p. 406)

Jobs listened to his muses which led him on a path of freedom, sometimes destruction, and always continual re-creation. He was polarizing, which could sometimes stifle his effectiveness, but he continually worked to "connect the dots looking forward" (Stanford Commencement Address). While he wasn't always popular and though he could alienate himself from his closest associates, he tried to live a genuine life of self-creation. In doing so, he created products and a company that can best be described in the most existentialist of terms: authentic.

15
Did Steve Jobs Live and Work for You?

Alexander R. Cohen

In his 2005 Stanford commencement speech, Steve Jobs offered a vision of work focused on love and personal satisfaction:

> Your work is going to fill a large part of your life, and the only way to be truly satisfied is to do what you believe is great work. And the only way to do great work is to love what you do. If you haven't found it yet, keep looking. Don't settle.

This message is one of the most inspiring things about Steve Jobs. It's a challenge: Pursue your happiness by doing work you love. If you find the right work, you can do great things. But are you entitled to organize your career around the pursuit of your own happiness? The government's response to one of Steve Jobs's last triumphs suggests it doesn't think so.

In July 2013, Denise Cote published an exciting tale of business adventure. It was the story of how Steve Jobs was able to stand up at the iPad launch and challenge Amazon's control of the ebook market. And it was the story of Apple executive Eddy Cue's three-month campaign to rescue the publishing industry and give his "seriously ill" boss one of his last successes (p. 30). But Denise Cote is not a journalist or a historian. She's a federal judge, and her purpose was to show that Jobs, Cue, and Apple had violated antitrust law (*United States v Apple Inc. et al.*).

Apple's still fighting, and Judge Cote's ruling may eventually be overturned. But Cote's story and her conclusion that what Apple did was illegal illustrate the essence of antitrust law: the principle that businessmen are not entitled to dedicate their work to the pursuit of their own happiness—that when their own goals conflict with what would best serve the consumer, they must sacrifice those goals.

$9.99 and Bust

Before Apple entered the ebooks business, the major publishers were scared. Amazon, which had introduced an ebook reader called the Kindle, sold almost ninety percent of all ebooks (p. 14). It sold many of the most popular ones for $9.99—one-third of the hardcover price in some cases. The publishers thought this low price was taking sales away from their hardcover books (which were more profitable), endangering bricks-and-mortar bookstores (which sold many of their physical books), and convincing customers that books simply weren't worth more (poisoning the market for hardcovers). Worst of all, they feared that if Amazon remained the main place readers went for ebooks, Amazon would start getting ebooks directly from authors—eliminating the role of publishers altogether (p. 16).

Amazon was able to sell the publishers' ebooks for $9.99 because the publishers were selling the books to Amazon on what's called a *wholesale model*. That is, the publishers sold ebooks to retailers for a set price per copy and allowed the retailers to set their own retail price (p. 14). Thus it was the publishers themselves who gave Amazon what it needed to threaten them: without the publishers' consent, Amazon could neither sell their ebooks nor set the price for them. But there were limits to what the publishers could do about it: each publisher feared retaliation if it stood too strongly against Amazon.

The publishers told Amazon they thought $9.99 was a problem. They even tried raising the wholesale price of some ebooks over $9.99. But Amazon stuck to its $9.99 price, even when that meant taking a loss (p. 17). Several publishers resorted to delaying the release of some ebooks until after the hardcovers had been out for a while, even though this led to piracy and lost sales (p. 25).

iPrice

"In 2009," Judge Cote wrote, sounding—not for the only time—remarkably like an Apple fan, "Apple was close to unveiling the iPad. With this revolutionary tablet, Apple was able to contemplate the arrival of its first great device for reading e-books" (p. 27). And a "great e-reader" was what Steve Jobs required before he'd take his company into the ebook market. So in November 2009, Jobs authorized Eddy Cue to start work on an iBookstore—and try to have it ready in time for Jobs's dramatic iPad launch, which had already been set for January 27th 2010 (p. 27). Cue scheduled meetings in New York.

Apple knew the publishers were trying to escape from $9.99, and it knew it needed a large catalog of ebook titles to make the iBookstore a success. So Cue walked into his negotiations with the publishers offering to sell ebooks for as much as $14.99 (pp. 31–32). Apple also said, however, that it "cannot tolerate a market where the product is sold significantly more cheaply elsewhere," and that unlike Amazon, it wasn't willing to sell ebooks at a loss (p. 33). Cue and two colleagues met with each publisher separately, but followed a script with each one (p. 33). Some of the publishers, for their part, discussed their negotiations with Apple with one another (p. 36).

After its initial meetings, Cue and his team returned to Cupertino and chewed over the situation. They considered a proposal for wholesale ebook prices based on wholesale physical-book prices (p. 37). But Cue instead chose to take up a proposal from two publishers, Hachette and HarperCollins: Apple would sell its ebooks on the *agency model*, just as it sold apps. It wouldn't pay a wholesale price, and it wouldn't set a retail price. Instead, it would let the publishers set the retail prices, and it would keep 30 percent as a commission. But to avoid being "embarrassed" by "unrealistically high prices," it would impose price caps (pp. 38–39). Those price caps, minus 30 percent, meant that Apple would pay less per ebook than Amazon was paying.

And one more thing. "Apple, quite simply, did not want to compete with Amazon on price" (p. 50). So Apple demanded a "most favored nation" clause that said it could match any other retailer's low price for a given ebook, at least if that ebook was a new release (p. 47). That effectively forced the publishers to move the other retailers to agency, since otherwise Amazon could have kept its $9.99 price and Apple could have matched it—and unlike Amazon, which had to pay the wholesale price even for ebooks it sold at a loss, if Apple sold an ebook for $9.99, it would get to keep 30 percent of that and give the publisher only $7 (p. 53).

With sixteen days remaining before the launch, Apple sent around its draft agreement. It told the publishers that it would insist on one set of terms for all publishers, and it confronted the publishers with a difficult choice: accept the lower revenues offered under the Apple agency contract, or turn down the chance "to confront Amazon as one of an organized group of Publishers united in an effort to eradicate the $9.99 price point" (pp. 51–52). As Cue warned Penguin: "There is no one outside of us that can do this for you. If we miss this opportunity, it will likely never come again" (p. 118). The publishers pushed back hard on the amounts of the price caps: they knew they were setting the new prices for ebooks. They pushed back on Apple's commission, too. But they didn't much resist the MFN clause, which would make sure they all moved Amazon to agency (pp. 55–65).

Cue went to New York one more time and didn't return till the day before the launch. As he brought one publisher after another on board, he kept the others apprised of his progress: he knew they needed the strength of numbers. When he found HarperCollins intransigent, he suggested

Jobs get in touch with James Murdoch of that publisher's parent, News Corp.

Jobs did. In an email, he told Murdoch that Apple "doesn't want to make more than the slim profit margin it makes distributing music, movies, etc." He said Amazon's model, in which the distributor took losses, "isn't sustainable for long." He said four of six publishers were already with Apple. And he gave this warning: "We will sell more of our new devices than all of the Kindles ever sold during the first few weeks they are on sale. If you stick with just Amazon, B&N, Sony, etc., you will likely be sitting on the sidelines of the mainstream ebook revolution" (pp. 79–80).

On January 27th, when Jobs launched the iPad, the iBookstore was ready to show. In his presentation, Jobs identified the five publishers participating; HarperCollins was among them. And he demonstrated how easy it was for an iPad user to buy a bestseller (p. 85).

But that bestseller's price caught a reporter's attention: Why, asked the reporter, would anyone buy an ebook for $14.99 from Apple that Amazon was offering for $9.99? "The price will be the same," said Jobs.

Macmillan told Amazon that if it didn't switch to agency, Macmillan new releases wouldn't be released for the Kindle. Amazon retaliated by taking the buy buttons off Macmillan books, both print and Kindle. But then four other publishers made the same demand, and Amazon capitulated—and wrote to Washington (pp. 87–90).

Once Apple and Amazon were both selling ebooks on the agency model, the five publishers raised the prices of most of their bestselling ebooks to the caps Apple had negotiated—"just," said Judge Cote, "as Apple expected" (p. 94).

The Law

The federal government sued and won. It's not clear from Judge Cote's opinion whether Amazon's letter, which was sent to the Federal Trade Commission, led to the lawsuit, which was filed by the Department of Justice.

Judge Cote found that Apple had rescued the publishers from the $9.99 price point they feared—and that this was illegal. What made Apple's actions illegal, Judge Cote found, was that the publishers—who were competitors—worked together to set prices, and that Apple participated in that cooperative action. (The publishers were sued too; they settled.)

"Apple's participation in the conspiracy proved essential," said Judge Cote.

> It assured each Publisher Defendant that it would only move forward if a critical mass of the major publishing houses agreed to its agency terms. It promised each Publisher Defendant that it was getting identical terms in its Agreement in every material way. It kept each . . . apprised of how many others had agreed to execute Apple's Agreements. As Cue acknowledged at trial, "I just wanted to assure them that they weren't going to be alone, so that I would take the fear awa[y] of the Amazon retribution that they were all afraid of." . . . Working against its own internal deadline, Apple achieved for this industry in a matter of weeks what the Publisher Defendants had been unable to accomplish for months before Apple became their partner. (pp. 117–18)

And what's wrong with that? "Consumers suffered in a variety of ways from this scheme to eliminate retail price competition and to raise e-book prices," said Judge Cote. Some consumers paid more to get the ebooks they wanted; others, to save money, missed out on the ebooks they wanted (p. 98).

But notice that consumers—ebook readers like you and me—didn't lose anything we already had. If you had already bought an ebook at $9.99 and the price went to $12.99, $3 didn't disappear from your bank account and the book didn't disappear from your Kindle. All that happened was that the publishers decided they were no longer willing to sell us any more of their products on Amazon's terms. You and I were perfectly free to decide that we weren't willing to buy ebooks at the new prices.

Those are the sorts of decisions people make in a free market: as producers they set the prices they're willing to sell for; as consumers they decide whether to buy things at the offered prices. And normally, that's perfectly legal. But in this case, by co-operating to raise prices instead of each trying to take the others' customers by lowering prices, the publishers (with Apple's help) took away something antitrust law says we should have had: the benefit of competition.

As Apple points out in its appeal, it sounds odd to say that Apple eliminated competition. After all, Amazon dominated the ebook market before Apple entered. As we usually use the word *competition*, Apple didn't destroy competition in ebooks—if anything, it introduced it!

But in antitrust law, *competition* is a technical term. What antitrust lawyers mean by competition is not that every business has competitors. Rather, a classic text defines competition as any situation where a judge can't make consumers better off by issuing a court order (Robert H. Bork, *The Antitrust Paradox*, p. 51). Thus "competition" can co-exist with monopoly—as long as the monopoly retains its status by serving its customers well, not by engaging in "anticompetitive behavior" a judge could order it to stop. And thus "competition" can be absent even while customers have a choice among what would normally be called competing businesses—in this case, the publishers—if the businesses engage together in "anticompetitive behavior," that is, activity that makes customers worse off than they might otherwise be. In this case, the publishers worked together to raise prices, which no one publisher would have been able to do alone.

Technically, Judge Cote classified what the publishers had done as a conspiracy among rival firms to fix prices. Such conspiracies are considered illegal by nature because the courts have held they're always or almost always bad for consumers. Judge Cote also found that even if what Apple and the publishers did didn't fall under that legal rule, it was still anticompetitive, because "the Agreements did not promote competition, but destroyed it. The Agreements . . . removed the ability of retailers to set the prices of their e-books and compete with each other on price, relieved Apple of the need to compete on price, and allowed the Publisher Defendants to raise the prices for their e-books" (p. 121).

By striving to force businesses to maximize their benefits to consumers, antitrust law takes a stand on a fundamental question of economic life: *whom do businesses exist to serve?* Antitrust says: businesses exist to serve the consumer—unless the government says otherwise.[1]

But when people like Steve Jobs create businesses, is their goal to serve the consumer? In a sense, of course it is: As William R Thomas points out in Chapter 8 of this book, businesses make money by providing customers products and services that enrich their lives. Whatever other goals a businessman has, such as making money or bringing a beautiful new technology into existence, he's not in business unless providing value to paying customers is central to his plan.

But antitrust demands more than that: after all, if customers hadn't found value in ebooks worth paying the new prices for, they wouldn't have paid, and that would have made the publishers lower their prices. Antitrust is designed to make businesses benefit consumers, not just as a means to their other goals, but even when this gets in the way of their other goals. In this case, antitrust demanded that the publishers serve consumers even though that meant not fighting back against what the publishers saw as a serious threat to their business.

And yet, the publishers—I hope—had, like Steve Jobs, chosen the work they loved. The publishing business was where they sought their happiness. Amazon, they thought, threatened that—and antitrust told them they could not join forces to fight back, could not stand as a unified group against the unified threat they faced. Their best shot at pro-

---

[1] Why the exception? Under the "state action" doctrine, if a state legislature excludes competition, that's legal, even though ordinarily federal laws like antitrust trump state laws. That shows that the fundamental moral principle of antitrust is that businesses exist to serve whatever goals are chosen by government—and that when no other goal has been chosen, the default goal is improving consumer welfare.

ductive happiness might be destroyed—as a sacrifice to low prices and to their customers.

Market Values

Many libertarians and conservatives defend a more-or-less unregulated market on the ground that by freely producing and trading, businessmen help others. That fits rather neatly with the ethical ideas of altruism (which holds that we must make the benefit of others the goal of our actions) and utilitarianism (which holds that we should seek to produce benefits without regard to who gets the benefits, ourselves or others). On these views, individuals aren't entitled to focus on their own happiness simply for their own sakes: if the publishers are allowed to remain in business, or if Steve Jobs is allowed to build his business and make a fortune, it's because that's good for others, or for people in general.

On such a view, antitrust makes sense. Yes, it interferes with people's freedom to run their businesses, but it shapes the market in such a way as to make it do a better job of producing value for customers. Or at least it's supposed to. So it's not surprising that some individuals and organizations commonly considered pro-market support antitrust. The classic text whose definition of "competition" I mentioned was written by Robert Bork, who ended his career associated with the American Enterprise Institute, still working on antitrust law.

But there's another defense of free enterprise. That argument holds "that your life belongs to you, and that the good is to live it" (Ayn Rand, "This Is John Galt Speaking," p. 120). Because you should live for yourself, it holds, you have the right to pursue your own happiness. You have the rights to liberty and property because you need those rights in order to create what you need in order to live and to be happy. Government must uphold those rights for you and everyone else because each of us needs those rights. And each of us should seek values from others by offering value in exchange and gaining agreement to trade, because when we deal by trade we recognize that each of us is entitled to pursue his own good. This is the view introduced by Rand. Jobs did not embrace Rand's political views, but if you are inspired by his challenge to find the work you love and achieve great things in it, you should consider what a philosophy that affirms your right to your own life and the value of productive achievement can offer you.

On that view, the antitrust laws are deeply unjust. If people should live for themselves, then regardless of whether raising prices was good for consumers, the publishers were right to try to figure out what was best for them and do it. Steve Jobs and Eddy Cue were right to pursue what they thought was best for Apple. And you have the same right to pursue your own happiness in your own life.[2]

---

[2] This chapter was written as part of the author's work as managing editor of the Business Rights Center and associate scholar at The Atlas Society.

16
Jobs and Heidegger Square Off on Technology

CHRISTOPHER KETCHAM

Somewhen in the hereafter . . .

I tune into the Eternal Network, EtN . . . The camera follows Walter Cronkite to center stage and the assembled audience claps politely. Cronkite takes a seat in a tall swivel chair and begins to speak towards Steve Jobs and Martin Heidegger.

CRONKITE: Welcome to tonight's *Walt Talks*, a discussion about technology. The participants for this event are Dr. Martin Heidegger, professor emeritus of Freiburg University in Germany and author of a dozen texts in philosophy and most notably for his influential work, *Being and Time,* a book that reconsiders the issue of being as situated in the world. From this and other works during his lifetime he considered how humans incorporate technology into their day to day lives to where it becomes so practical it is like part of the hand. But Dr. Heidegger is also concerned that our tendency towards ever more consumption of technology requires thinking about humans and human needs first." [*Slight applause; Heidegger nods but does not smile under his brushy moustache*].

CRONKITE: Our second participant is Steve Jobs, co-founder and former CEO of Apple Computer which was instrumental in introducing the personal computer into daily life. Later, Apple evolved to produce smaller and more portable personal technical devices such as the iPod music device, the multi-faceted iPhone, and then the multi-media tool, the iPad. But Mr. Jobs has also said that much of technology has not been designed with human sensibilities in mind." [*Polite applause. Jobs has an eerie almost beatific staring smile.*]

CRONKITE: The panelists and this moderator have agreed to limit the discussion to technology. Therefore we will not address personal issues, management styles, or topics outside the narrow realm of technology unless there is a direct tie to the issues of and meaning of technology in our daily lives and into our eternal future both here and for our loved ones back on Earth. The panelists each will be given time to make an opening statement. I will then ask a question to each panelist. Before the event Mr. Jobs was chosen by lottery to speak first. Mr. Jobs, please make your opening remarks.

It's All Shit

JOBS: Most technology is shit. You wouldn't want it anywhere near you, yet you buy this shit every day and ignore its shittyness. Why do you run like lemmings to the next and even buggier version of cheap software and even cheaper equipment that runs it?

We have lost the heart of the design, all in the effort to get cheaper, cheaper, cheaper. 'I end up not buying a lot of things because I find them ridiculous.' Ridiculous because of design, yes design. People say that I obsess about design and that's true. Once my family was going to purchase a washer and dryer. It was the topic of conversation for days at our dinner table. What, in fact, did we want? Did we want to save time, save money, save the planet, or have soft clothes? We got what we wanted because the manufacturer put some thought into the design of the machine, not just threw something together without thinking of the humans who would use it.

JOBS: [*Pulls an iPod from his pocket and holds it out towards the audience in his palm.*] Look at this. What is it and what is it supposed to do? Does it have all sorts of slots and cords and wires and buttons? No, it has a simple purpose and design. Its sole purpose is to hold and play thousands of songs and other music. It doesn't need to rip and burn new songs, that's for other devices. So the buttons are simple. Scroll the ball for the song you want and press or simply do this and have the songs play randomly. But it is also seamlessly integrated with your Mac when you want more or different music.

But technology isn't just about functionality. I could have designed this as a round disc, made it look like a beer coaster. Instead, consider its clean lines, its seamless construction, its pure white color. It's a work of art don't you think? It's technology revealing the beautiful from within the utility of technology. It's an iPod, or a Macintosh, or an iPhone or iPad, something that has taken advantage of the unconcealed nature of the purposing of the device. It takes, as Dr. Heidegger calls it, its enframing to a new level, a level where technology becomes the essence of the responsibilities that were required to come together to make this thing both useable and pleasing to the eye. Technology can be art and we at Apple have always shown that art can be good technology.

And how does this happen? It's a process of thinking down the technology to its essence and most minimum essentials, making it simpler and simpler, finding the simplest functions for the product that you want to make. And remember, always remember . . . 'We make tools for people. Tools to create; tools to communicate. The age we're living in, these tools surprise you . . . That's why I love what we do. Because we make these tools, and we're constantly surprised with what people do with them.' While I may be putting words in the doctor's mouth, I think that he. like me, will say that 'design is the fundamental soul of a man-made creation that ends up expressing itself in successive outer layers of the product or service.'

185

Listen, we didn't have to design the inside of the first Mac as carefully as we did the outside. Nobody will see it. But it's the soul of the item that's at stake and the soul of mankind both for the maker and the user that is important. Design is a pedigree that is wound through the product or service. If you peel back the layers of the iPod you'll see design after design after design decision. Each design decision depends upon its integration and synergy with other design decisions. But this is not a static thing, for the entire design must be rethought, even changed when there is a conflict in the hierarchy or we discover some new thing that will make the design better. When we made new versions of the iPod we didn't just hammer the new feature on, we redesigned the whole device and thought through all of the issues again.

'Look at Mercedes's styling, the proportion of sharp details to flowing lines. Over the years they made the lines softer but the details starker.' That's what we did starting with the Mac when I returned to Apple. And this same attention to detail flowed into the iPod and other products.

The essence of technology is design. So I ask the world, please stop making shit.

It's a Question of Technology

CRONKITE: Thank you Mr. Jobs. Dr. Heidegger, your opening remarks.

HEIDEGGER: My question is: What is technology and our relationship to it? For this it is necessary to explore the essence of technology which is not as some would guess, technological. 'Everyone knows the two statements that answer our question. One says: Technology is a means to an end. The other says: Technology is a human activity. The two definitions of technology belong together.' But is this all there is to technology? No it is not enough, for that we must look more closely at the elements that make up technology, for example, one of Mr. Jobs's iPods. Let's begin with means and causes.

All means have causes. Aristotle tells us that there are four causes of the iPod Mr. Jobs is holding in his hand."

[*With a piercing stare, Jobs holds the iPod out towards the audience in the same manner as when he introduced the product at the Apple Music Festival in 2001.*]

HEIDEGGER: [*Looks over at Jobs, studies his face for a moment, and continues.*] The first is, it is made from metal, plastic, and glass. The second is the form that it takes, an electronic device, a rectangle with rounded edges but wafer thin. The third is its use as a repository for music and an amplifier to present the music for your listening enjoyment. And the fourth is its maker, the technicians at Apple who made it. But is this all that there is to the technology of the iPod? No, because the four causes work together, belong together and in synergy become *responsible* for producing something beyond the four causes lined up in a row.

There are four responsibilities associated with these causes. First, the iPod owes its being as an electronic device to the metal, plastic, and glass, but it is also indebted to the iPodness of the iPod: it could be nothing other than what it is, an iPod. And there is a third responsibility, its purpose, and that's for you to store and listen to music. And for the fourth responsibility there is the iPod maker. It was Mr. Jobs's thinking about the purposes and aesthetics and functionality that were co-responsible with the other three responsibilities.

But what unites these responsibilities as iPod? It is the responsibilities that set the thing in motion *towards* becoming the iPod. I call this *motion towards* 'a presencing', a bringing forth of iPodness which is not yet there . . . but which is always arising out of itself. Place all the components for the iPod on the table. What do you see? An array of components? Of course. Now begin to assemble the iPod and suddenly it starts to metamorphose into something more than just parts and pieces.

But how does this bringing forth happen? The four causes by themselves do not reveal the technology as the iPod. It is the bringing forth from the combinatory nature of the four forces that unconceals and *reveals* iPodness. 'What has the essence of technology to do with revealing? The answer: everything. For every bringing-forth is grounded in revealing.' The bringing forth gathers within itself the four modes of responsibility and within this revealing makes them reveal something which was not evident before.

Technology is not just means and ends; on the contrary it is revealing. And so is modern technology a revealing as in the case of the iPod. 'Unlocking, transforming, storing, distributing, and switching about are ways of revealing. But the revealing never simply comes to an end.'

This revealing is important because technology has its own standing, a standing in reserve. The jet on the runway conceals its purposes but is already standing in reserve for its purposes. By concealing, for example, consider the boy who sees this jet in the runway for the first time. He may not understand that it flies or that it carries passengers, but you and I know it stands in reserve for just those purposes.

Who accomplishes the standing reserve? 'Obviously, man. To what extent is man capable of such a revealing? Man can indeed conceive, fashion, and carry through this or that in one way or another. But man does not have control over un-concealment itself, in which at any given time the real shows itself or withdraws.' Therefore, and once again, the reveal, the un-concealing, comes from the interrelation of the four causes and their synergistic combination of responsibilities.

Man does not will iPodness; it comes from the un-concealing. The reveal and the standing reserve are not the essence of technology. Technology's essence begins with its *enframing*. 'In enframing, that un-concealment comes to pass in conformity with which the work of modern technology reveals the real as standing-reserve.' 'We are questioning concerning technology in order to bring to light our relationship to its essence. The essence of modern technology shows itself in what we call enframing.' But enframing is not the whole answer to the question concerning technology. Within the revealing is revealed what we might call the essence of freedom—the freeing of technology to be revealed, to reveal itself. The revealing is in the open which is the essence of freedom; however that which frees what has been freed is always concealed.

When you purchase the iPod how much time do you spend thinking about all that went into its design and manufacture? Probably little, and that massive effort to produce the iPod is not revealed even when you examine the product carefully. But when we consider the essence of the iPod we experience a sense of wonder at its simplicity, its size, and its usefulness, already in that we are experiencing its destiny towards a revealing. 'In this way we are already sojourning within the open space of destining, a destining that in no way confines us to a stultified compulsion to push on blindly with technology or, what comes to the same thing, to rebel helplessly against it and curse it as the work of the devil.

Quite the contrary, when we once open ourselves expressly to the essence of technology, we find ourselves unexpectedly taken into a freeing claim.' Freeing yes, but the reveal is also a danger, a danger that the un-conceal will be misinterpreted or misapplied. The danger is not the technology itself, it is the enframing. 'All essencing endures. But is enduring only permanent enduring? Does the essence of technology endure in the sense of the permanent enduring of an Idea that hovers over everything technological, thus making it seem that by technology we mean some mythological abstraction?' Of course not.

Technology's essence lets itself be seen when it is revealed as, for example, the iPod. We can deconstruct or even reverse engineer the device but what would that do to the revealing of the iPod? And by analogy say we dissected a living being what would be lost? Rightly so, its essence.

But essence as revealed can be for good or for ill. Uranium was revealed by man both in its peaceful use and destructive use. Both enframings permanently endure; the bomb device cannot be un-enframed. But are these the only purposes for uranium? It is the enframing as a single way of revealing that is dangerous because it can restrict our freedom, conceal our free essence in deference to the enframed thing.

'So long as we represent technology as an instrument, we remain held fast in the will to master it. We press on past the essence of technology.' So what is the essence of technology? In a sense the answer is ambiguous, it is the mystery of revealing, of revealing truth. The danger is the saving, the saving of power, the least expense for the greatest profit. Technology has, for the most part, lost its aesthetic. It is the savings that are produced that are sending us down the path to think of technology's essence as usefulness only and not its aesthetic qualities, the art of its revealing. So we reveal only what is the barest utility of the thing and the beauty that is concealed in the essence of technology remains concealed.

Is It Necessary?

CRONKITE: Thank you Dr. Heidegger. Now onto individual questions. Mr. Jobs, the question that many are asking is whether the iPod, iPhone, or iPad are necessary devices at all. And, within this question is another which asks whether technology from the personal computer forward has made people more impersonal, communicating by distance rather than face-to-face.

JOBS: None of it, none of what Apple made is necessary, not like food, air, and water. We only made life simpler. It's about opportunity. The world has become smaller, more interconnected, not less so. We have always communicated by distance: letters, telegraph, telephone. Technology took letters and made them electronic by marrying word processing with the internet. Phones became portable so instead of waiting to talk to someone when a fixed phone is available, you can now pull a phone from your pocket, talk, and continue on to your destination. We didn't invent the mobile phone, we made it more useful.

The Japanese built transistor radios in the 1960s and Sony the Walkman in the 1980s. But the music industry was so insular and so bent on protecting their copyrights from pirates they lost sight of what their customers wanted—their own music libraries on demand when and where they wanted and mixed to what they want to hear at the moment they want to hear it. You know it took us a long time to bring the record execs kicking and screaming to the table. Finally they agreed that they had no clue how to do this and we showed them how with the iTunes store.

So, maybe nothing we have done is necessary, but when people saw what they could do with the product and how well it worked and looked, they became opportunists for themselves. People see the value in technology that values them, their needs, their time, their interests. Necessity, not like air and food, but improving their daily lives.

Have we done this? Absolutely. Have we made communication impersonal? I'm not so sure. The shy are emboldened by texting and tweeting. The proliferation of communication methods like blogs and Facebook have provided new ways for people to communicate interpersonally and from the heart more than perhaps in any other generation. That said, will communication be relegated to texts and selfies and from one box to another? No, technology will find a way to bring back the face-to-face in a way that seems as real as if the other is standing right here in the room.

Luddites, Unite

CRONKITE: Thank you, Mr. Jobs. Dr. Heidegger some accuse you of being a Luddite, a hater of technology and that you would prefer us to return to a more primitive state of being. How do you respond?

HEIDEGGER: Certainly technology has led humanity to do some horrible things to the world and to each other. But it's not my project to criticize such things. It's for others to assess the moral worth or depravity of individual technologies. What I am concerned about is that we can lose ourselves, our being, our humanity, in technology if we are not careful.

Your question to Mr. Jobs was prescient. Have we become so enamored with technology in itself that it already has replaced some aspects of being human? Are we letting technology do the talking where we simply respond to its capabilities without considering our own need for being in the world with others? Are we still the masters of technology or has technology begun to master us? Does technology diminish our humanness, take away valuable abilities of thinking and doing? What will this mean for us as beings in the world? Can technology solve all of our problems; replace us even or most of what we would call our being? This is the question that we should be asking: How do we continue to develop technology that un-conceals our being and humanity without blindly replacing those aspects of our being in an enframing that diminishes what it means to be human?

But it is also as Mr. Jobs has said—because it can be done more cheaply, it doesn't have to be done without consideration of aesthetics. And if part of the condition of being human is recognizing the beauty of the world we live in then should not part of technology's agenda be towards making the useful also something we want to use because it complements our world?

So, you see, it's not about producing the most for the least. Mr. Jobs has shown that his products, while they cost more, are often easier to use and are more pleasant to behold and be with than something similarly functional but poorly designed and cheap. Are we wanting to do more and more and more for less and less without considering whether more for less is better?

There is a balance that's required, a balance between what of our work technology replaces and how technology does this without depreciating humanity. In other words, is the utility worth the price of the change in our lives? And there is the balance of utility and beauty which brings us back to the essence of the thing. Does its utility, its functionality, and design comport with what our conception to be human really is? In other words is it like the Greek temple, does the wonder and the grandeur of this technology enhance what it is to be human and advance our culture, or is it the tasteless box on the hill that has the same utility but does nothing to advance our culture?

CRONKITE: Thank you Dr. Heidegger and thank you Mr. Jobs for your comments and ideas this evening. And that's the way it is today in the world of technology. [1]

---

[1] The content of Jobs's ideas given in this program is mainly derived from Walter Isaacson, *Steve Jobs*. The content of Heidegger's ideas comes mainly from his essay, "The Question Concerning Technology." Actual direct quotations, shown here in single quotes, come from the book edited by George Beahm, *I, Steve Jobs: Steve Jobs in His Own Words* and from "The Question Concerning Technology."

Martin Heidegger joined the Nazi party before World War II and was sympathetic to Hitler. His recently released *Black Notebooks* also suggest that he was anti-Semitic. Some want to ignore all of his writings because of this; others want to separate his philosophy from his political ideology. Only his views on technology and its relationship to humanity are the subject of this program. You be the judge of whether his views on technology should be considered or discarded. Steve Jobs's brusque and even cruel management style and his complicated personal life and habits sometimes overshadowed his technological accomplishments. Only his views on technology are discussed in this program. Again, you be the judge of whether his views are worthwhile or not.

17
Simplicity Is the Ultimate Sophistication

DENNIS KNEPP

New York's Museum of Modern Art (MoMa) has several Apple computers, including the original 1984 Macintosh. These computers are not used by the museum; they are part of the museum's collection because of their design.

The Macintosh has the look of the modern while other computers from the same time look old. The Macintosh was a huge success and much of that is due to the look of it. Other computers of the time were big clunky boxes while the Macintosh looked like a friendly face. There is a subtle forehead above the screen and the disk slot formed an off-centered smirk. It even smiled at you when you turned it on.

Other computers were intimidating while the Macintosh was inviting. The handle on top asks you to touch it and pick it up. Steve Jobs encouraged his team to design with a principle from Leonardo da Vinci: "Simplicity is the ultimate sophistication" (*Steve Jobs*, pp. 79–80). The Graphic User Interface with a mouse meant that the user didn't need to know complex computer codes. It was easy to use, like an appliance. The Macintosh bridged the gap between art and technology, it was popular among college students in the humanities, and the huge catalogue of artistic fonts provided an artistic outlet for anyone making a word document. The flier for your high-school club could now be in Comic Sans.

Despite the success of the Macintosh, Jobs left Apple under duress in 1985 and pursued his sophisticated simplicity design aesthetic under his new company: NeXT. He believed that his design philosophy had been stifled in Apple. People disagreed with him. There were shouting arguments. But with NeXT, Jobs would be free to express his design philosophy. There would be no barriers now. Jobs believed that being able to truly express his successful philosophy of simple sophistication would create an even bigger success.

It didn't happen. The NeXT Cube was a failure. How could this happen? It doesn't seem to make any sense. The principle of simple sophistication worked so well with the Macintosh design despite the fighting with others at Apple. It would seem that the same principle of simple sophistication would work *even better* without the fighting in his new company. Jobs thought it would. That's why he did it, but it didn't work.

Jobs tried to design the NeXT as a simple cube, but this simple cube design made the NeXT computer so expensive that no humanities college student could ever afford to buy one. The Macintosh made modern art accessible to the masses while the NeXT Cube did not, even though Jobs was using the same design principle of simple sophistication. Why did it work in one but not the other? How is it that freely following his design principle led to its failure?

I believe that an answer can be found with Slavoj Žižek's reading of Georg Wilhelm Friedrich Hegel (1770–1831). In brief, the failure of the NeXT Cube design is a symptom of the contradictions already found in the Macintosh design. "Simple sophistication" is a contradictory principle. This principle was successfully expressed in the design of the Macintosh while Jobs was stifled by the constraints of working at Macintosh; but the freedom of expression allowed in NeXT meant that the contradictions of his design principle could be fully expressed in the failure of the NeXT. Hegel argues that this kind of problem is found everywhere: positive ideas are later revealed to lead to be their own negation. The positive idea can only be regained by starting again just as Jobs had to start again at Apple for his next success with the iMac. The Mac, NeXT, iMac develop dialectically.

The traditional understanding of Hegel's dialectical logic is in terms of thesis, antithesis, and synthesis. There's an idea (thesis), and then the opposite of that idea (antithesis), and then the two are brought together into something greater (synthesis). The 2011 biography by Walter Isaacson presents Jobs's story in three acts: Act I is the success of the Macintosh; Act II is the excesses of the NeXT Cube; and Act III is the culmination in the iMac (p. 219). The traditional version of the Hegelian dialectic would have the Macintosh as thesis, NeXT as antithesis, and iMac as synthesis. But this theory fails because the NeXT is not the opposite of the Macintosh; the NeXT design is *more* of the Macintosh design. Jobs was able to follow his design philosophy *even more* with NeXT. The problem here is with the traditional understanding of Hegel's logic. A better theory is presented by Slavoj Žižek in his 2013 book *Less than Nothing: Hegel and the Shadow of Dialectical Materialism*. The original positive idea is contradictory and unstable. The second idea as a negation is a symptom of this contradictory instability. The third idea is actually a starting again for the first idea. To understand why Hegel thinks that contradictions are found everywhere requires some background in Kant.

From Kant to Hegel to Jobs

Hegel is the culmination of a significant era in the history of philosophy—German Idealism—which lasted from the 1787 publication of Kant's *Critique of Pure Reason* to Hegel's death from cholera in 1831. German Idealism includes the writings of Fichte, Schelling, and others, but "It all really begins with Kant, with his idea of the *transcendental constitution of reality*" (Less than Nothing, p. 9). Immanuel Kant (1724–1824) argued in his *Critique of Pure Reason* that there is the world of appearances and the world of things themselves. We can only have knowledge of the world of appearances—what Kant calls the "phenomenal world." We can never know reality itself independent of appearances.

Kant was trying to eliminate metaphysical speculation. "Metaphysics" is the study of reality itself. It literally means the study of theory that's beyond physics. For example: was the universe created at some time or has the universe always existed? This is a question that is "beyond physics" and so metaphysical philosophers think that they can answer this question one way or another just by thinking about it really hard. Kant argued that this is impossible because each side can be proven. A philosopher can prove that the universe was created at some time and can prove that the universe has always existed. Kant called these opposing arguments "antinomies" and declared that metaphysics was impossible because of them. But Hegel took a different lesson and argued that the antinomies of reason are necessary for doing metaphysics. The world itself is full of these tensions and the dialectical unfolding of them is what drives world history. The Hegelian dialectical logic shows how reality itself is driven by these oppositions.

Isaacson's biography *Steve Jobs* has many examples of startling oppositions starting with the fact that Steve Jobs had two sets of parents. His biological parents were college educated and insisted that their son become college educated. His adoptive parents were not college educated and, in fact, his adoptive father was "a high school dropout with a passion for mechanics" (*Steve Jobs*, p. 3). So, his parents were both college educated and not college educated. Jobs grew up in Santa Clara Valley of South Bay San Francisco, what we now call "Silicon Valley." It was an opposition of both agricultural orchards and high-tech industry. It was both peaceful hippies and a front line in the Cold War. A teenage Steve Jobs worked at a communal apple orchard while his friend the twenty-two-year old Steve Wozniak landed at job at Hewlett-Packard designing calculators (*iWoz*, p. 122).

The name "Apple Computer" is a representation of these oppositions: both high tech and organic; both counterculture and mainstream; both art and technology. Here's biographer Walter Isaacson:

> Apple. It was a smart choice. The word instantly signaled friendliness and simplicity. It managed to be both slightly off-beat and as normal as a slice of pie. There was a whiff of counterculture, back-to-nature earthiness to it, yet nothing could be more American. And the two words together—Apple Computer—provided an amusing disjuncture. (Walter Isaacson, *Steve Jobs*, p. 63)

The "Apple" is also evocative of Jobs's fruitarian diets. Steve Jobs followed ascetic diets of simplicity and restriction and often he ate nothing but fruit. Isaacson relates the following interview with Jobs's daughter, Lisa:

> Even at a young age Lisa began to realize his diet obsessions reflected a life philosophy, one in which asceticism and minimalism could heighten subsequent sensations. "He believed that great harvests came from arid sources, pleasure from restraint," she noted. "He knew the equations that most people didn't know: Things led to their opposites." (p. 260)

This is a clear statement of Jobs's belief in creativity driven by opposites and this is visually manifested in the design of the Macintosh.

Macintosh Simplicity

Steve Wozniak is the genius engineer who built the first Apple computer: the first computer with a screen and a keyboard. Wozniak is an introvert and Jobs is an extrovert. They are opposite personalities and yet they were able to overcome this and design our modern world. Steve Wozniak was such an introvert that starting his senior year in high school he would spend hours alone in his bedroom designing computer hardware (*iWoz*, pp. 54–55). Because he couldn't afford the chips, he designed simpler versions: "I had a hunch after a year or so that nobody else could do the sorts of design tricks I'd come up with to save parts. I was now designing computers with half the number of chips the actual company had in their own design, but only on paper" (p. 55).

Steve Wozniak eventually built his compact computers: "I mean, we'd actually built a computer from scratch and proved that it was possible—or going to be possible—for people to have computers in a really small space" (pp. 88–89). Previously all computers had switches and lights like a dashboard in a cockpit, like the helm in *Star Trek*, or like the control panels on the Death Star in *Star Wars*: all lights, switches, dials, knobs. Steve Wozniak built the first computer with a screen and a keyboard: "Before the Apple I, all computers had hard-to-read front panels and no screens and keyboards. After Apple I, they all did" (p. 158).

The Macintosh with its graphic user interface and mouse is the culmination of their modern user-friendly compact personal computer. Steve Jobs's design influences include growing up in an Eichler home that is designed to be "simple and clean modernism produced for the masses" (*Steve Jobs*, p. 125). He drew inspiration from Bauhaus and Zen Buddhism. (See Chapter 10 in this volume.) This simplicity starts with a small footprint, no bigger than a phone book, which forced the engineers to put the screen on top of the computer, making the Macintosh taller and more head-like (p. 128).

> Jobs kept insisting that the machine should look friendly. As a result, it evolved to resemble a human face. With the disk drive built in below the screen, the unit was taller and narrower than most computers, suggesting a head. The recess near the base evoked a gentle chin, and Jobs narrowed the strip of plastic at the top so that it avoided the Neanderthal forehead that made the Lisa subtly unattractive. (*Steve Jobs*, p. 129)

The Macintosh was designed first, and only then did the engineers get the hardware inside. Jobs argued with his design team that the Macintosh should be classic like a Porsche rather than voluptuous like a Ferrari (p. 128). They made numerous plaster models and argued about them at length. Jobs would argue "Great art stretches the taste, it doesn't follow tastes," and challenged them to make a computer as simple and intuitive as a Cuisinart (pp. 128–29).

The Macintosh also had a handle on top which invited you to pick it up. The handle would probably be used rarely or maybe even only once. But the handle wasn't really about functionality. The handle was designed to make the Macintosh more friendly. Other computers were intimidating and not something you'd touch unless you had to, but the handle invited you to touch the Macintosh and this made it more personal and friendly.

Here is the best statement of their belief that the Macintosh was art:

> When the design was finally locked in, Jobs called the Macintosh team together for a ceremony. "Real artists sign their work," he said. So he got out a sheet of drafting paper and a Sharpie pen and had all of them sign their names. The signatures were engraved inside each Macintosh. No one would ever see them, but the members of the team knew that their signatures were inside, just as they knew that the circuit board was laid out as elegantly as possible. Jobs called them each up by name, one at a time. . . . Jobs waited until last, after all forty-five of the others. He found a place right in the center of the sheet and signed his name in lowercase letters with a grand flair. Then he toasted them with champagne. "With moments like this, he got us seeing our work as art," said Atkinson. (Walter Isaacson, *Steve Jobs*, p. 134)

The Macintosh is art. It belongs in MoMa.[1] They were right to sign their art. But the contradictions that created it

---

[1] <www.moma.org/search/collection?query=macintosh+computer>. Thank you to Libby Sullivan, Faculty Librarian at Big Bend Community College, for help with this reference.

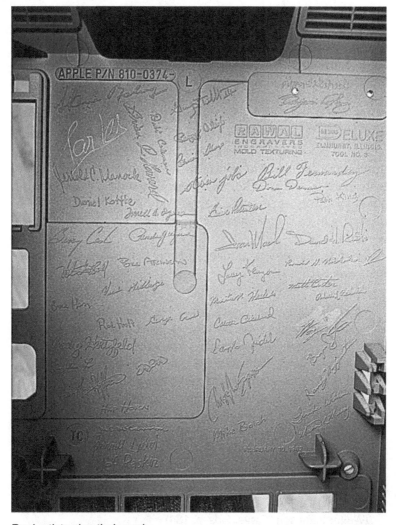

Real artists sign their work.
<http://en.wikipedia.org/wiki/Macintosh_128K#mediaviewer/File:Apple_
Macintosh_128Kb_naked.jpg>

can be found even in Steve Jobs's signature. Children sign
their names with lower case letters. And yet this childish approach is done with a cursive "grand flair" that is beyond any
childish signature.

The NeXT Negation

The company isn't "Next" it's "NeXT" and the capital XT shouts: *we are designed*. The NeXT logo itself is evidence that Jobs is going too far. The logo is on a black cube that looks three dimensional. The top face has the logo and is tilted. A red "N" and a yellow "e" are the first row with a green "X" and a purple "T." This is a lot in a logo, but then Jobs did pay $100,000 for it. The designer was Paul Rand, the "dean of corporate logos" with "fifty years" of experience.

> On the final spread, Rand presented the logo he had chosen. "In its design, color arrangement, and orientation, the logo is a study in contrasts," his booklet proclaimed. "Tipped at a jaunty angle, it brims with the informality, friendliness, and spontaneity of a Christmas seal and the authority of a rubber stamp." The word "next" was split into two lines to fill the square face of the cube, with only the "e" in lowercase. That letter stood out, Rand's booklet explained, to connote "education, excellence . . . e = mc^2." (*Steve Jobs*, p. 220)

"e" can also mean "excess." Here are the elements of the Macintosh, such as friendliness, taken too far into their own negation. The NeXT logo tries so hard to be friendly that it is no longer friendly.

The NeXT was envisioned as a high-end academic research tool but the price caused by the designs put it out of range of most academics. Jobs wanted a cube. A simple perfect cube. Jobs insisted that every angle be precisely ninety degrees which made it nearly impossible to manufacture and when they did figure out how to make it with two molds there was a seam left where the two halves came together. A seam is a blemish on this perfect cube and so Jobs insisted that the die caster start again and a more expensive method was invented for the cast and a more expensive sanding machine was purchased to remove the lines (pp. 222–23). Jobs insisted on a matte black finish and this made the imperfections show up even more. The desire to mass produce a simple and sophisticated black cube collapses into itself.

Perfection can inspire us but it cannot be obtained. Jobs also took his adopted father's advice of the importance of the unseen parts to its negation: "He made sure that the screws inside the machine had expensive plating. He even insisted that the matte black finish be coated onto the inside of the cube's case, even though only repairmen would see it" (p. 223). All of this resulted in delays and expense. The original plan was to release the NeXT Cube computer in spring of 1987 for $3,000 but it was delayed until 1989 and carried the steep price of $6,500. According to the Inflation Calculator on dollartimes.com, that would be $12,571.10 in 2014 dollars.

The Macintosh was simple and sophisticated modern design for the masses but the same aesthetic principles are taken to their own negation in the NeXT so that none of the masses could afford it. It was time to try again.

Second Chance at Apple

Steve Jobs returned to Apple in 1997 as an "interim CEO." The title "iCEO" is so appropriate given that Jobs oversaw the design of the iMac, iTunes, iPod, iPhone, and iPad. The iMac is the visual expression of the dialectic of the Macintosh and the NeXT. It's both and neither at the same time. The Macintosh is preserved even in the name "iMac"— "Mac" is a clear reference to the name "Macintosh" and a signal of continuity. Furthermore, the iMac design is similar to the Macintosh design in that it is a small computer with a friendly design and a handle that invites your touch. NeXT also is preserved in the name "iMac" by using a lower case vowel in an unconventional location to reference, in this case, the Internet. The NeXT design is preserved in the use of color on the iMac case and a well designed interior that used NeXT hardware. But the iMac is also neither a Macintosh or a NeXT. The iMac was something more. Here's biographer Isaacson on the design of the iMac:

Once again Jobs had produced an iconic new product, this one a harbinger of a new millennium. It fulfilled the promise of "Think Different." Instead of beige boxes and monitors with a welter of cables and a bulky setup manual, here was a friendly and spunky appliance, smooth to the touch and as pleasing to the eye as a robin's egg. You could grab its cute little handle and lift it out of the elegant white box and plug it right into a wall socket. People who had been afraid of computers now wanted one, and they wanted to put it in a room where others could admire and perhaps covet it. "A piece of hardware that blends sci-fi shimmer with the kitsch whimsy of a cocktail umbrella," Steven Levy wrote in *Newsweek*. (Walter Isaacson, *Steve Jobs*, p. 355)

I love this description of the iMac. It certainly captures my experience as an iMac user. And there are so many new contradictions: both a high-tech appliance and as natural as a robin's egg; both the virtue of conquering fear and the vice of inspiring coveting; and the *Newsweek* quotation: "A piece of hardware that blends sci-fi shimmer with the kitsch whimsy of a cocktail umbrella." Hegel's radical thesis is that the world itself is contradictory and this can be seen even in design of the iMac.

The first success of the Macintosh led to the negation in the NeXT which led to Jobs's second career at Apple and success with the iMac. Žižek writes that it is necessary to fail the first time and try again:

> The lesson of repetition is rather that our first choice was necessarily the wrong one, and for a very precise reason: the "right choice" is only possible the second time, for only the first choice, in its wrongness, literally creates the conditions for the right choice. The notion that we might have already made the right choice the first time, but just blew the chance by accident, is a retroactive illusion. (Slavoj Žižek, *Less than Nothing*, p. 465)

And so here's the answer to our first question. The principle of sophisticated simplicity in the Macintosh was revealed to be flawed by the negation of the NeXT which made it possible to try again with a new positive design in the iMac.[2]

_____

[2] Thank you to two English instructors from Big Bend Community College: Cara Stoddard for reminding me to read Žižek and John Carpenter for editorial help.

Insanely Great Inspiration

Here are brief sketches, listed chronologically, of some of the thinkers mentioned in this book. These thinkers are the inspiration for many of the ideas in the foregoing chapters, as well as in our civilization. You should also look at the References beginning on page 221 below.

Buddha (around 563–483 B.C.E.)

Siddhārtha Gautama is commonly known as the Buddha which means "the enlightened one." Born in India, his teachings became the foundations of Buddhism, one of the world's major religions.

The core of these teachings is the Four Noble Truths: the existence of suffering, the cause of suffering, the possibility of restoring well-being, and the Noble Eightfold Path for the ending of suffering and the attainment of Enlightenment.

Unlike Abrahamic religions, Buddhism is primarily concerned with the individual's enlightenment. The Buddha did not endorse belief in any gods or other supernatural phenomena.

Plato (427–347 B.C.E.)

Plato is the most influential and best known philosopher of the Western tradition. According to the outstanding twentieth-century philosopher Afred North Whitehead, "the safest general characterization of the European philosophical tradition is that it consists of a series of footnotes to Plato."

Plato wrote dialogues—discussions between his teacher Socrates and various other Greeks with a range of different opinions. These dialogues present Plato's views on the nature of reality, knowledge, art, ethics, and the state. The most famous of these are the *Republic* (about the ideal form of government) and the *Apology* (about Socrates's trial for impiety).

Plato is what philosophers call an idealist—he argues that reality consists in abstract ideas or forms and that the world we perceive and live in is but a reflection of this true reality. This conception is memorably presented in Plato's celebrated Allegory of the Cave.

Aristotle (384–322 B.C.E.)

A student of Plato, Aristotle is sometimes referred to simply as "The Philosopher." He was the first to formalize reasoning into the discipline of logic. More empirically minded than Plato, Aristotle rejected Plato's idealism, arguing instead that true reality is in the concrete, particulars, not abstract ideas.

Aristotle wrote treatises spanning many areas of knowledge, including biology, art, psychology, ethics, politics, physics, and mathematics. His ideas dominated medieval European thinking and are still influential today.

St. Thomas Aquinas (1225–1274)

Aquinas is the most famous and influential of the Scholastic philosophers. Aquinas drew directly upon Aristotle, and upon the Muslim writer Averroes (ibn Rushd) and the Jewish writer Maimonides (Moshe ben Maimon), both of whom worked to integrate Aristotle into their respective religious traditions.

Aquinas's ideas (known as 'Thomism') were not recognized by the Church when he was alive, and were sometimes condemned. His insistence on logic—for example that God could not perform the logically contradictory, and that the existence of God could be proved by reason alone—was felt to be dangerous. But Aquinas was made a saint fifty years after his death and later became completely respectable, and then the single officially approved philosophy of the Church.

Among Aquinas's achievements were his Five Ways (of proving the existence of God), his analysis of just and unjust wars, and his development of 'natural law' as the basis for human community life, law, and ethics. Politically, he favored monarchy, defended slavery, and endorsed the use of violence against heretics. His most important writings are *Summa Theologica*, *Summa contra Gentiles*, and his commentaries on Aristotle.

Much philosophical thinking after the fifteenth century is a critical reaction against the Scholasticism embodied in the writings of Aquinas.

Thomas Hobbes (1588–1679)

Although writing in the seventeenth century, English philosopher Thomas Hobbes's thought is decidedly modern in many ways. He is best known for his political philosophy expounded in *Leviathan* (though he also developed a materialist theory of the physical world).

Hobbes's political philosophy is focused on creating and maintaining social and political order. In order to avoid the chaos and insecurity of what he called the state of nature, Hobbes argued that we ought to submit to the power of an absolute sovereign who will make all political decisions.

Although few today accept Hobbes's conclusions, his arguments are still widely influential in contemporary political philosophy.

René Descartes (1596–1650)

The seventeenth-century French philosopher René Descartes challenged Scholasticism, the dominant philosophy of medieval Europe, and introduced methods and concepts that still frame contemporary philosophy.

Descartes is best known for his argument for certainty based on *The Cogito*. The Cogito, "Cogito ergo sum," is the proposition that translates as "I think, therefore I am." Descartes decided, as an exercise, to try to doubt everything he believed. He argued that there was just one thing he could not doubt: his own existence, since he was continually aware of his thoughts. From this, by an extended process of reasoning, he derived the existence of the physical world and of God.

Descartes is also known for mind-body dualism: the theory that the mental and the physical are entirely distinct and dissimilar substances. So, subjective mental events such as thoughts and feelings are not physical and belong to the soul.

His most important works are his *Discourse on the Method* and *Meditations*.

John Locke (1632–1704)

John Locke's life was bound up with the revolutions in England in the seventeenth century and his writings helped form the thinking of the American revolutionaries. Locke is generally regarded as the key figure in the foundation of classical liberalism: private property, limited government, and the free market. He argued against the theory of absolute monarchy and in favor of religious toleration. His influence can easily be seen in such documents as the US Declaration of Independence. Thomas Jefferson considered Locke one of the three greatest men of all time (the other two being Francis Bacon and Isaac Newton).

In his *Second Treatise of Government* (1689), Locke maintained that the true function of government is to protect individuals' rights, notably their property rights.

His greatest work, *An Essay concerning Human Understanding*, argues for the philosophical theory known as empiricism: that knowledge is based on the evidence of our senses.

David Hume (1711–1776)

David Hume was a Scottish philosopher renowned for his work in epistemology and ethics. His *Treatise of Human Nature* (1740) is generally acknowledged to be the most brilliant work of pure philosophy ever written in English.

Skeptical of our ability to know anything for certain, Hume challenged the standard accounts of perception, knowledge, causality, and ethics. He questioned the assumption that ethics could be derived from factual descriptions of the world; no set of affairs in the world can by itself entail any particular moral judgment—this is the famous problem of 'ought' and 'is'. Instead, he maintained that we are motivated to act by our emotional responses, in particular, sympathy.

Like his English predecessor Locke, Hume was a classical liberal whose ideas on morality, law, government, and economic life influenced the American Founders.

Adam Smith (1723–1790)

Although best known as the father of economics, Adam Smith was first and foremost a moral philosopher. In his *Theory of Moral Sentiments*, Smith defended a view of human virtue grounded in sympathy and pleasure. He argued that it is through seeing, even experiencing, the painful or pleasurable effects of our actions on others that we develop the virtues necessary both for living well with others and for leading a happy life of our own.

In *An Inquiry into the Nature and Causes of the Wealth of Nations*, Smith founded 'political economy' (now called economics) by bringing together and developing everything that was then known about the theory of economic life. Smith outlined the social and political requirements necessary for a free and prosperous society, and argued for free trade.

Together, these two great works of Smith present a systematic understanding of human nature and peaceful social interaction.

Immanuel Kant (1724–1804)

Immanuel Kant was a German philosopher who revolution-ized modern philosophy. His work in metaphysics and epis-temology made previous philosophical points of view seemingly irrelevant. Rather than seeing our knowledge and minds as passively conforming to external reality, Kant ar-gued that our minds must play an active role in creating our picture of reality. He advanced the highly controversial view that such basic categories as space, time, and causation are not derived from experience, but are inherent in the mind, so that we are unable to think outside of them.

Kant's ethics has also been influential. His ethics is called 'deontological', meaning that it is not based on evalu-ating the consequences of actions, but rather on whether ac-tions conform to basic moral rules and whether a person adopts those rules with a good will. He formulated the Cat-egorical Imperative that prescribes the only appropriate reason for acting: "Act only according to that maxim by which you can at the same time will that it should become a universal law."

Politically, Kant was a liberal who argued for the freedom of the autonomous individual to decide upon his own beliefs and actions without being subject to any authority.

Jeremy Bentham (1748–1832)

Jeremy Bentham was an English philosopher and reformer best known for his formulation of the principle of the utility: the greatest happiness for the greatest number. One of the founders of Utilitarianism, Bentham argued that the test of right or wrong was whether an action or policy produced greater happiness for more people than the alternative.

As a radical reformer in eighteenth- and nineteenth-cen-tury England, Bentham advocated social policies such as freedom of expression, equal rights for women, and economic freedom because he claimed they would produce the greatest happiness for the greatest number.

Georg Wilhelm Friedrich Hegel (1770–1831)

Notoriously hard to understand, Georg W.F. Hegel was a German philosopher who developed a comprehensive philosophical system that explained civilization in terms of the historical developments of ideas. His absolute idealism attempted to make sense of reality as a whole that included both subject and object. He also developed a kind of dialectical reasoning that sought to make sense of oppositional ideas as new unified concepts. His views influenced Karl Marx and generations of Continental philosophers.

Ralph Waldo Emerson (1803–1882)

A uniquely American thinker, Ralph Waldo Emerson was a popular and influential essayist and lecturer in the nineteenth century. The leader of the Transcendentalist Movement, he spoke out against slavery and criticized popular religion. His essays put forward an optimistic and romantic vision of the individual. His essay "Self-Reliance" is still widely read and anthologized.

John Stuart Mill (1806–1873)

Like his mentor and contemporary Jeremy Bentham, John Stuart Mill was an English philosopher and reformer. He articulated his version of ethical philosophy in his famous work *Utilitarianism*. Unlike Bentham who treated all pleasures as equal, Mill distinguishes between different kinds of pleasure. This meant that some pleasures could count more when subjecting one's actions to the principle of utility.

In his *On Liberty* Mill presented a robust defense of individual freedom and his *The Subjection of Women* provided one of the first calls for full legal and moral equality of women.

Søren Kierkegaard (1813–1855)

One of the fathers of Existentialism, the Danish philosopher Søren Kierkegaard wrote largely on questions of religion and human freedom. Kierkegaard focused on the individual and the choices and commitments the individual made, in particular regarding one's faith. He explored the nature of emotions, such as despair, angst, and love.

Kierkegaard is also well-known for his three stages of individual development: the aesthetic, the ethical, and the religious.

Karl Marx (1818–1883)

Best known as the co-author, with Friedrich Engels, of the *Communist Manifesto* (1848), Karl Marx developed an influential theory of political economy that called for radical changes to the structure of economic and political life. According to Marx, different classes in society have different and conflicting interests. He argued that history is best understood as a history of these class conflicts.

Although trained as a philosopher, Marx's great four-volume work, *Capital*, is a work of economic theory, in which he criticizes apologists for capitalism and looks forward to its replacement by communism. Marx tried to show that the workers create all economic value, and that the employer's or investor's profit is due to a part of the workers' labor that is not recompensed. Because of capitalism's inherent instability, increasing monopolization, and the growing power of the workers, Marx expected that capitalism would be abolished and replaced by communism, a system in which there would be no private property and in which the state would gradually cease to exist.

Marx is well-known for the theory called 'historical materialism': that changes in technology give rise to changes in the economy, which then gives rise to changes in the whole culture.

Marx's ideas have had little impact on economics or philosophy, but considerable impact on history and sociology.

William James (1842–1910)

William James was an influential professor of psychology and philosophy at Harvard University.

A central figure in American Pragmatism, James articulated a radical view of knowledge and truth. An idea was true, he argued, if we could both incorporate it into our current manner of thinking and show its usefulness in our lives.

He is also well known for his examination and explanation of religious experience in *The Varieties of Religious Experience*.

Friedrich Nietzsche (1844–1900)

Friedrich Nietzsche was a German philosopher whose writings challenged, and continue to challenge, the philosophic mainstream. He famously declared that "God is dead" and criticized religion, Christianity in particular, at its core. His ethics can either be read as a kind of nihilism or as a radical call for self-realization and self-affirmation. Considered by some to be one of the fathers of Existentialism, Nietzsche's writings were more literary than those of other philosophers.

Nietzsche was deeply concerned with authenticity and meaning in one's life and less concerned about a consistent and systemic approach to knowledge.

His most famous works are *Thus Spoke Zarathustra*, *The Gay Science*, and *Beyond Good and Evil*.

Maria Montessori (1870–1952)

One of the most influential thinkers on education, the Italian-born physician and educator developed a systematic method and curriculum based on her close observations and study of children learning. She argued that children naturally learn in reaction to their environment. The role of the educator is thus first to remove obstacles to this process and second to fashion the child's environment to facilitate his or her development.

Her method is still widely used in many schools throughout the world.

Joseph Schumpeter (1883–1950)

Joseph Schumpeter declared that his ambitions had been to become the greatest economist in the world, the greatest horseman in Austria, and the greatest lover in Vienna—and that he had fulfilled two of these three (he did not specify which).

Schumpeter is best known to the general public for his book *Capitalism, Socialism, and Democracy* and to economists for his two-volume *Business Cycles.* He argued that capitalism would be so successful it would lead to the creation of an intellectual class that would seek capitalism's destruction, and a culture which would be unfavorable to entrepreneurship, capitalism's driving force.

Though he was pessimistic about the future of capitalism because of his dim view of the intellectuals, Schumpeter argued that through constant innovation and entrepreneurship, capitalism, if it were allowed to, could continue to flourish and improve everyone's lives indefinitely.

Schumpeter famously invented the term "creative destruction" to characterize the ceaseless process of innovation and entrepreneurship which drives progress.

Martin Heidegger (1889–1976)

One of the most controversial and influential philosophers of the twentieth century, Martin Heidegger is a key figure in the philosophical movements known as phenomenology and existentialism.

Heidegger's most famous work, *Being and Time,* is an attempt to explain human beings in terms of their fundamental existence in time. He was also concerned with what would make one's life truly authentic. His philosophy is often challenging and frequently confounding, but Heidegger's notorious support of Nazism remains his most disturbing legacy.

Jean-Paul Sartre (1905–1980)

Jean-Paul Sartre was a leading French existentialist and phenomenologist, whose work primarily focused on the individual's radical freedom of action and the correlative responsibility that comes with that freedom.

Sartre maintained that freedom is inescapable—we are "condemned to be free," but most people deceive themselves in an attempt to evade this freedom and responsibility, so that they end up living inauthentic lives. His most important philosophical work, *Being and Nothingness*, is an attempt to explain human beings in terms of the relationship between consciousness and reality.

Sartre was also an outstanding novelist and playwright. His greatest works are *Nausea*, *The Age of Reason*, and *No Exit*.

Ayn Rand (1905–1982)

The Russian-born novelist-philosopher was the author of two of the best-selling books of all time, the novels *The Fountainhead* and *Atlas Shrugged*. Her fiction and non-fiction writings present her philosophical views which are broadly based in the Aristotelian tradition.

Atlas Shrugged describes what happens when the small number of creative geniuses—entrepreneurs, engineers, scientists, and artists—decide to withdraw from society, in effect going on strike.

Rand argued for realism and reason in metaphysics and epistemology, moral individualism in ethics, and libertarianism in political philosophy.

Philippa Foot (1920–2010)

Philippa Foot was a British philosopher best known for her work in ethics. She helped to revive interest in Aristotle's ethics as part of contemporary Virtue Ethics. In *Natural Goodness*, her last published work, she sets out a defense of morality that is grounded on human nature and practical reason. Her influence in contemporary ethics is largely based on her enduring critiques of dominant ethical viewpoints, namely non-cognitivism and consequentialism.

Israel Kirzner (1930)

The English-born economist is an emeritus professor of economics at New York University. He is best known for his work on entrepreneurship.

The entrepreneur in Kirzner's view plays an essential role in markets by discovering and developing untapped opportunities. Kirzner is critical of dominant viewpoints in more mainstream economics that often rely on static mathematical models and ignore the indispensable role of the entrepreneur.

John R. Searle (1932)

The American philosopher, John Searle, teaches at UC Berkeley and is best known for his contributions to philosophy of language and philosophy of mind. He made his reputation with his theory of speech acts; speech acts are utterances (such as saying "I do" at the appropriate time in a wedding ceremony) that are actions doing something in the world (making you married).

His Chinese Room thought experiment, first published in the early 1980s, spawned a cottage industry in philosophy, with thousands of publications attacking and defending it. The thought experiment is intended to counter various claims made about artificial intelligence. So-called "Strong AI" holds that, with sophisticated enough programming, computers would be able to achieve real understanding.

The Chinese Room thought experiment shows that one might be able to manipulate symbols and produce meaningful statements (by following a set of defined rules) without actually understanding the symbols or the statements. Searle does not rule out the possibility that it might one day be feasible to construct machines which could attain consciousness, thus being able to understand and to think, but insists that this has not yet happened, and cannot happen merely by any amount of increase in information-processing capability.

Peter Singer (1946)

Peter Singer is one of the best known and most influential contemporary philosophers. He is most famous for his 1975 book, *Animal Liberation,* which argues that we have no rational basis for excluding non-human animals from our moral considerations.

Using utilitarianism as his ethical foundation, Singer's work focuses primarily on applied ethics issues like abortion, euthanasia, and world poverty. He is widely criticized for many of his views, including his view that human infants lack personhood.

Singer maintains, in *The Life You Can Save* and other works, that comfortably off individuals in affluent societies are morally obliged to cut their living expenses down to subsistence and to donate most of their incomes to the relief of poverty. In the volume *Singer Under Fire*, Peter Singer responds to various attacks by critics.

Slavoj Žižek (1949)

A cultural critic, Marxist philosopher, and popularizer of philosophy, Slavoj Žižek garners a wide popular following and broad influence. His work focuses on ideology and argues that our unconscious motives are active in constructing reality.

Žižek writes widely and entertainingly on topics ranging from movies and pop culture to psychoanalysis and religion.

References

Acemoglu, Daron, and Simon Johnson. 2005. Unbundling Institutions. *Journal of Political Economy* 113:5.

Adams, Scott. 2012. Reality Distortion Field. *The Scott Adams Blog* (April 18th),
<http://dilbert.com/blog/entry/reality_distortion_field/>.

Aquinas, Thomas. 2003. *On Law, Morality, and Politics*. Second edition. Hackett.

Aristotle. 1963. Nicomachean Ethics. In R. Bambrough, ed., *The Philosophy of Aristotle*. New American Library.

———. 1980. *The Nicomachean Ethics*. Oxford University Press.

Barber, Benjamin. 1995. *Jihad vs. McWorld*. Random House.

Barboza, David. 2011. Apple Cited as Adding to Pollution in China. *New York Times*
<www.nytimes.com/2011/09/02/technology/apple-suppliers-causing-environmental-problems-chinese-group-says.html>.

Barrett, William. 1958. *Irrational Man: A Study in Existential Philosophy*. Doubleday.

Baumol, William. 1990. Entrepreneurship: Productive, Unproductive, and Destructive. *Journal of Political Economy* 98:5.

Beahm, George. 2011. *I, Steve Jobs: Steve Jobs in His Own Words*. Kindle Edition (Online: B2 Books).

Becker, Ernest. 1973. *The Denial of Death*. Simon and Schuster.

Bentham, Jeremy. 1988. *The Principles of Morals and Legislation*. Prometheus.

Bernstein, Andrew. 2013. *Heroes and Hero Worship*. Taped lecture. Ayn Rand Institute.

References

Biddle, Craig. 2002. *Loving Life: The Morality of Self-Interest and the Facts that Support It*. Glen Allen Press.

Binswanger, Harry. 2014. *How We Know: Epistemology on an Objectivist Foundation*. TOF Publications.

Bork, Robert H. 1978. *The Antitrust Paradox: A Policy at War with Itself*. Basic Books.

Bray, Nicholas. 2011. The DNA of the World's Most Innovative Companies. INSEAD (July 21st).

Brennan, Chrisann. 2013. *The Bite in the Apple: A Memoir of My Life with Steve Jobs*. St. Martin's.

Brin, Sergei, and Larry Page. 2004. Google Founders Talk Montessori. <https://www.youtube.com/watch?v=0C_DQxpX-Kw>.

Burlingham, Bo, and George Gendron. 1989. The Entrepreneur of the Decade. Interview with Steve Jobs. *Inc.*, <www.inc.com/magazine/19890401/5602.html>.

Campbell, Joseph. 2008. *The Hero with a Thousand Faces*. New World Library.

Churchland, Paul M. 2013. *Matter and Consciousness*. MIT Press.

Coreless, Roger J. 1989. *The Vision of Buddhism*. Paragon House, 1989.

Cringely, Robert. 1996. *Triumph of the Nerds*. TV movie. PBS.

Csikszentmihalyi, Mihaly. 1996. *Creativity: Flow and the Psychology of Discovery and Invention*. HarperPerennial.

Descartes, René. 1993. *Meditations on First Philosophy*. Hackett.

———. 2008. *A Discourse on the Method*. Oxford University Press.

Deutschman, Alan. 2001. *The Second Coming of Steve Jobs*. Broadway.

Dilger, Daniel. 2012. Tim Cook Exposes the Lie that Steve Jobs Ignored Philanthropy. *Apple Insider*. <http://appleinsider.com/articles/12/02/02/tim_cook_exposes_the_lie_that_steve_jobs_ignored_philanthropy_.html>.

Dormehl, Luke. 2012. *The Apple Revolution: The Real Story of How Steve Jobs and the Crazy Ones Took Over the World*. Virgin.

Douglass, Frederick. 1860. The Trials and Triumphs of Self-Made Men. *Frederick Douglass Papers* 3.

Downie, R.S. 1969. Collective Responsibility. *Philosophy* 44.

Dudrow, Andrea. 2000. Notes from the Epicenter: Exploring the Reality Distortion Field. <www.creativepro.com/article/notes-epicenter-exploring-reality-distortion-field>.

Dyer, Jeffrey, Hal Gregersen, and Clayton Christensen, *The Innovator's DNA*. Harvard Business Review Press.

References

Elkind, Peter. 2008. The Trouble with Steve Jobs. *Fortune*, <http://archive.fortune.com/2008/03/02/news/companies/elkind_jobs.fortune/index.htm>.

Emerson, Ralph Waldo. 1883. Self-Reliance. In *Essays by Ralph Waldo Emerson: First and Second Series Complete in One Volume*. Houghton, Mifflin.

Entrepreneur. 2014. Steve Jobs: An Extraordinary Career. *Entrepreneur*, <www.entrepreneur.com/article/197538>.

Foot, Philippa. 2003. *Natural Goodness*. Oxford University Press.

French, Peter. 1979. The Corporation as a Moral Person. *American Philosophical Quarterly*.

————. 1984. *Collective and Corporate Responsibility*. Columbia University Press.

————. 1995. *Corporate Ethics*. Harcourt, Brace.

Frost, Robert. 1960. The Road Not Taken. In Edward Connery Lathem, ed., *The Poetry of Robert Frost*. Holt, Rinehart, and Winston.

Fumerton, Richard. 1990. *Reason and Morality*. Cornell University Press.

Fung, Brian. 2013. OS X Mavericks Shows Apple Loves Clean Designs, Even if You Can't See Them. *Washington Post* (October 22nd).

Gallo, Carmine. 2009. *The Presentation Secrets of Steve Jobs: How to Be Insanely Great in Front of Any Audience*. McGraw-Hill.

Gardiner, Bryan. 2007. Apple Kills Think Secret: Publisher Nick Ciarelli Talks. *Wired*, <www.wired.com/2007/12/apple-and-think/>.

Garside, Juliette. 2013. Child Labour Uncovered in Apple's Supply Chain. *The Guardian*, <www.theguardian.com/technology/2013/jan/25/apple-child-labour-supply>.

Greta, Andrew. 2011. The Individualist. In Luskin and Greta 2011.

Guilar, Joshua, and Karen Neudorf. 2014. Steve Jobs: A Practicing Buddhist, an Entrepreneur, and an Innovator. *Buddhism and Australia*, www.buddhismandaustralia.com/index.php/articles/articles-2012/116-steve-jobs-a-practicing-buddhist-an-entrepreneur-and-an-innovator-joshua-guilar-and-karen-neudorf.html.

Gustin, Sam. 2012. Apple Agrees to Labor Reforms After 'Serious' Foxconn Violations. *Time*, <http://business.time.com/2012/03/29/apple-agrees-to-labor-reforms-after-serious-foxconn-violations>.

References

Hanh, Thich Nhat. 1999. *The Heart of the Buddha's Teaching: Transforming Suffering into Peace, Joy, and Liberation.* Broadway.

Heidegger, Martin. 1977. *The Question Concerning Technology and Other Essays.* Harper and Row.

Heritage.org. *2014 Index of Economic Freedom.* <www.heritage.org/index/pdf/2014/countries/china.pdf>.

Hertzfeld, Andy. 2005. *Revolution in the Valley: The Insanely Great Story of How the Mac was Made.* O'Reilly.

Herzing, D.L., and T.J. White. 1999. Dolphins and the Question of Personhood. *Special Issue: Etica Animali.*

Hicks, Stephen R.C. 2009. What Business Ethics Can Learn from Entrepreneurship. *Journal of Private Enterprise* 24:2.

Hill, Bob. 2009. Apple CEO Steve Jobs' "12 Rules of Success". *BusinessBrief.com* (September 9th 2009), <http://www.business-brief.com/apple-ceo-steve-jobs-12-rules-of-success/>.

Hobbes, Thomas. 1994. *Leviathan.* Hackett.

Hume, David. 1985 [1739]. *A Treatise of Human Nature.* Clarendon.

Hunt, Sarah, and Mimi O'Connor, directors. 2011. *Steve Jobs: One Last Thing.* Movie. Pioneer Productions, PBS.

Isaacson, Walter. 2011. *Steve Jobs.* Simon and Schuster.

James, William. 1981 [1907]. *Pragmatism.* Hackett.

———. 1982. The *Varieties of Religious Experience: A Study in Human Nature.* Penguin.

Jobs, Steve. 2005. Stanford Commencement Address. "You've Got to Find What You Love," Jobs Says. <http://news. stanford. edu/news/2005/june15/jobs-061505.html>.

Jobs, Steve, and David Sheff. 1985. *Playboy* Interview with Steve Jobs. *Playboy* (February 1st). Reprinted in *Playboy* 2012.

Johnson, Joel. 2011. 1 Million Workers. 90 Million iPhones. 17 Suicides. Who's to Blame? *Wired* (March).

Kant, Immanuel. 1945 [1785]. *Fundamental Principles of the Metaphysics of Morals.* Regnery.

———. 2009 [1785]. *Groundwork of the Metaphysics of Morals.* Harper.

Kierkegaard, Søren. 2006. *Fear and Trembling.* Cambridge University Press.

———. 1980. *The Essential Kierkegaard.* Princeton University Press.

Kinsley, Michael. 2009. The Warren & Bill Show. *Hedge Magazine* 13, <http://issuu.com/squareupmedia/docs/h_13>.

References

Kirzner, Israel M. 1973. *Competition and Entrepreneurship*. University of Chicago Press.

———. 1979. *Perception, Opportunity, and Profit: Studies in the Theory of Entrepreneurship*. University of Chicago Press.

Kling, Arnold, and Nick Schulz. 2011. *Invisible Wealth: The Hidden Story of How Markets Work*. Encounter.

Krainin, Julian, and Michael R. Lawrence, directors. 1990. *Memory and Imagination: New Pathways to the Library of Congress*. Documentary movie. Library of Congress.

LaFollette, Hugh. 2003. *The Oxford Handbook of Practical Ethics*. Oxford University Press.

Lillard, Angeline Stoll. 2008. *Montessori: TheScience Behind the Genius*. Oxford University Press

List, Christian, and Philip Pettit. 2011. *Group Agency: The Possibility, Design, and Status of Corporate Agents*. Oxford University Press.

Locke, John. 1980. *Second Treatise of Government*. Hackett.

———. 1996. *An Essay concerning Human Understanding*. Hackett.

Luskin, Donald L., and Andrew Greta, eds. 2011. *I Am John Galt: Today's Heroic Innovators Building the World and the Villainous Parasites Destroying It*. Wiley.

Marx, Karl H., and Friedrich Engels. 1994 [1848]. *The Communist Manifesto*, in *Karl Marx: Selected Writings*. Hackett.

Mayhew, Robert, ed. 2005. *Ayn Rand Answers: The Best of Her Q&A*. New American Library.

Mariotti, Steve. 2009. Entrepreneurship and Education. *Kaizen* 9. <http://www.ethicsandentrepreneurship.org/20091005/interview-with-steve-mariotti/>.

Markoff, John. 2011. Stephen P. Jobs, 1955–2011: Redefined the Digital Age as the Visionary of Apple (Obituary). *New York Times* (6th October 2011), p. A1.

Marty, Eduardo. 2011. Entrepreneurship in Argentina. *Kaizen* 15. <http://www.ethicsandentrepreneurship.org/20110221/interview-with-eduardo-marty/>.

Mill, John Stuart. 2007. *On Liberty and The Subjection of Women*. Penguin.

Nietzsche, Friedrich. 1974. *The Gay Science*. Random House.

———. 2012. *The Will to Power*. Aristeus.

North, Douglass. 1990. *Institutions, Institutional Change, and Economic Performance*. Cambridge University Press.

References

Peikoff, Leonard. 1991. *Objectivism: The Philosophy of Ayn Rand*. Meridian.

Petrilli, Michael J. 2012. Memo to the World: America's Secret Sauce Isn't Made in Our Classrooms. <http://edexcellence.net/commentary/education-gadfly-daily/fly-paper/2012/memo-to-the-world-americas-secret-sauce-isnt-made-in-our-classroom.html>.

Pita, Maria Isabel. 2009. *Concise Guide to Ancient Egypt's Magic and Religion*. Amazon Digital Services.

Pixar. Our Story. <www.pixar.com/about/Our-Story>.

Plato. 1997. *Republic*. In *Plato: Complete Works*. Hackett.

Plato. 2012. *The Republic*. Amazon Digital Services.

Playboy, ed. 2012. *Fifty Years of the Playboy Interview: Moguls*. Amazon.

Preston, Caroline. 2011. The Giveaway. *The Chronicle of Philanthropy*. <http://philanthropy.com/section/Home/172>.

Price, David A. 2008. *The Pixar Touch*. Knopf.

Quinton, Anthony. 1975. Social Objects. *Proceedings of the Aristotelian Society* 76.

Rahula, Walpola. 1974. *What the Buddha Taught*. Grove Press.

Rand, Ayn. 1961. *For the New Intellectual*. Signet.

———. 1961. This Is John Galt Speaking. In *For the New Intellectual*.

———. 1964. *The Virtue of Selfishness: A New Concept of Egoism*. Signet.

———. 1964. The Objectivist Ethics. In *The Virtue of Selfishness*.

———. 1967. *Capitalism: The Unknown Ideal*. Signet.

———. 1967. What Is Capitalism? In *Capitalism: The Unknown Ideal*.

———. 1984. *Philosophy: Who Needs It*. Signet.

———. 1984. The Metaphysical Versus the Man-Made. In *Philosophy: Who Needs It*.

Rasmussen, Douglas B., and Douglas J. Den Uyl. 1991. *Liberty and Nature: An Aristotelian Defense of Liberal Order*. Open Court.

———. 2005. *Norms of Liberty: A Perfectionist Basis for Non-Perfectionist Politics*. The Pennsylvania State University Press.

Rathunde, Kevin, and Mihaly Csikszentmihalyi. 2005. Middle School Students' Motivation and Quality of Experience: A Comparison of Montessori and Traditional School Environments. *American Journal of Education* 111 (May).

Rawls, John. 1971. *A Theory of Justice*. Harvard University Press.

Rogers, Everett M. 1962. *Diffusion of Innovations*. Free Press.

References

Rogers, Steven. 2002. *The Entrepreneur's Guide to Finance and Business*. McGraw-Hill.

Rogowsky, Mark. 2013. Apple's New iPads Show Company Believes It's Alone in the Tablet Market. *Forbes* (October 22nd).

Ronnegard, David. 2011. Corporate Moral Agency and the Role of the Corporation in Society. PhD Thesis, London School of Economics.

Roszak, Theodore. 1969. *The Making of a Counter Culture: Reflections on the Technocratic Society and Its Youthful Opposition*. Doubleday.

Salvino, Robert, Michael Tasto, and Gregory Randolph. 2014. *Entrepreneurial Action, Public Policy, and Economic Outcomes*. Edward Elgar.

Sanandaji, T., and P. Leeson. 2013. Billionaires. *Industrial and Corporate Change* 22:1.

Sartre, Jean-Paul. 1994 [1943]. *Being and Nothingness*. Gramercy.

Schaler, Jeffrey A., ed. 2009. *Peter Singer Under Fire: The Moral Iconoclast Faces His Critics*. Open Court.

Schlender, Brent. 1998. The Three Faces of Steve. *Fortune* (November 9th).

Schumpeter, Joseph A. 1950. *Capitalism, Socialism, and Democracy*. Third edition. Harper.

Searle, John R. 1980. Minds, Brains, and Programs. *Behavioral and Brain Sciences* 3.

———. 1984. *Minds, Brains, and Science: The 1984 Reith Lectures*. Harvard University Press.

———. 1992. *The Rediscovery of the Mind*. MIT Press.

Seligman, Martin E.P. 2012. *Flourish: A Visionary New Understanding of Happiness and Well-being*. Atria.

Sen, Paul, director. 2012. *Steve Jobs: The Lost Interview*. Movie. Magnolia Home Entertainment.

Simpson, Mona. 2011. A Sister's Eulogy for Steve Jobs. Delivered on October 16th 2011 at the Memorial Church of Stanford University. *New York Times* (October 30th).

Sims, Peter. 2011. The Montessori Mafia. *The Wall Street Journal Blogs*. <http://blogs.wsj.com/ideas-market/2011/04/05/the-montessori-mafia/>.

Singer, Peter. 1972. Famine, Affluence, and Morality. *Philosophy and Public Affairs* 1:3 (Spring).

———. 2009. *The Life You Can Save: Acting Now to End World Poverty*. Random House.

References

Smith, Adam. 1904 [1776]. *Wealth of Nations*. Methuen.
———. 2009. *The Theory of Moral Sentiments*. Liberty.
Smith, George H. 1979. *Atheism: The Case Against God*. Prometheus.
Smith, Tara. 2000. Money *Can* Buy Happiness. *Reason Papers* 26 (Summer).
———. 2006. *Ayn Rand's Normative Ethics: The Virtuous Egoist*. Cambridge University Press.
Solomon, Avi. 2012. Searching for Magic in India and Silicon Valley: An Interview with Daniel Kottke, Apple Employee #12. Boing-Boing <http://archive.is/20120916001330/http://boingboing.net/2012/08/09/kottke.html#selection-793.1-793.96>.
Strong, Michael, ed. 2009. *Be the Solution: How Entrepreneurs and Conscious Capitalists Can Solve All the World's Problems*. Wiley.
Stuart, Elizabeth. 2011. Steve Jobs's Philanthropy: Did He Give Anonymously or Not at All? *Deseret News*, <http://www.deseretnews.com/article/700187536/Steve-Jobs-philanthropy-Did-he-give-anonymously-or-not-at-all.html>.
Thurrott, Paul. 1998. Whoa! Apple announces the iMac. <http://windowsitpro.com/windows-server/whoa-apple-announces-imac>.
Ullekh, N.P. 2012. Steve Jobs Thought Apple Products, Not Charity, Would Help Lives: Walter Isaacson. *Economic Times*, <http://articles.economictimes.indiatimes.com/2012-10-11/news/34365188_1_walter-isaacson-isaacson-s-steve-jobs-apple-products>.
United States v. Apple Inc. et al., No. 12 Civ. 2826, 85 (S.D.N.Y. July 10, 2013). All citations to page numbers are to the official PDF version, <http://www.justice.gov/atr/cases/f299200/299275.pdf>.
Vascellaro, Jessica E. 2012. Turns Out Apple Conducts Market Research After All. <http://blogs.wsj.com/digits/2012/07/26/turns-out-apple-conducts-market-research-after-all/>.
Veatch, Henry B. 1962. *Rational Man: A Modern Interpretation of Aristotelian Ethics*. Indiana University Press.
Velasquez, Manuel. 2003. Debunking Corporate Moral Responsibility. *Business Ethics Quarterly*.
Wahl, Daniel. 2011–2012. The Patience of Jobs. *The Objective Standard* 6: 4 (Winter 2011–2012).
Weaver, William G. 1998. Corporations as Intentional Systems. *Journal of Business Ethics* 17.

References

Werhane, Patricia H., and R. Edward Freeman. 2003. Corporate Responsibility. In LaFollette 2003.

Whitehead, Alfred North. 1978. *Process and Reality*. Free Press.

Williamson, Claudia. 2009. Informal Institutions Rule: Institutional Arrangements and Economic Performance. *Public Choice* 139:3.

Yogananda, Paramhansa. 2005 [1946]. *Autobiography of a Yogi*. Crystal Clarity.

Young, Jeffrey S., and William L Simon. 2005. *iCon: Steve Jobs, The Greatest Second Act in the History of Business*. Wiley.

The A Players

CARRIE-ANN BIONDI is an Associate Professor of Philosophy at Marymount Manhattan College, in New York City. Her research interests include citizenship theory, patriotism, immigration policy, Aristotelian virtue ethics, children's rights, Socratic pedagogy, and *Harry Potter*. She also has over fifteen years of experience in professional editing, is Co-Editor-in-Chief (with Irfan Khawaja) of *Reason Papers*, and is proud of the fact that she wrote her dissertation on a Macintosh Performa 466.

ALEXANDER R. COHEN is a philosopher launching his own organization. He's also a freelance writer, editor, tutor, and book designer. Alexander edited the bestselling *Myths about Ayn Rand* and created Your Life Is Worth an Hour, a Facebook page that encourages people to help friends who are considering dying recapture the value of their lives. He has taught both law and philosophy at the undergraduate level for the City University of New York. Alexander earned his law degree at the University of Pennsylvania, where he was a member of the *Law Review*. He studied philosophy at CUNY, the University of Virginia, and the Atlas Society Graduate Seminar, where he later taught. Alexander is a Google fan and uses Windows, but he does use at least one apple product most days—usually from Mott's. He lives near New York City.

DANIELLE FUNDORA is an instructor at Rock Valley College, Illinois, where she teaches courses in philosophy and world religions. She credits her eight-year-old MacBook, "Phoebe," with providing both technological and emotional support in attaining her PhD at Arizona State University. Her philosophical interests include medical ethics, feminist epistemology, and breathlessly anticipating the next Mac operating system, "Mufasa."

STEPHEN R.C. HICKS is Professor of Philosophy at Rockford University, Illinois, and the author of *Nietzsche and the Nazis* and *Explaining Postmodernism: Skepticism and Socialism from Rousseau to Foucault.* He is also, perhaps hypocritically, one of the few contributors to this volume who has never owned an Apple product.

JASON IULIANO earned his JD from Harvard Law School and is now a PhD candidate in Politics at Princeton University where he is writing a dissertation on the moral and legal status of corporate persons. Hoping SIRI would have firsthand knowledge of the status of non-human persons, Jason asked her if she thinks that she is a person. SIRI coyly responded, "I think, therefore I am. But let's not put Descartes before the horse."

CHRISTOPHER KETCHAM is a reformed academic living in Pennsylvania, far from Silicon Valley. He is a writer on social justice, philosophy and popular culture, and risk management where he has edited and contributed to two books. Think about it, Jobs's connectivity technology of today has become just like Heidegger's nineteen-twenties hammer, just another extension of the hand. Left or right handed? It doesn't matter.

SHAWN E. KLEIN has taught philosophy at Rockford University, Illinois; Mesa Community College, Arizona; Marist College; and Mount Saint Mary's College, New York. He co-edited and contributed to *Harry Potter and Philosophy* (2004). He founded The Sports Ethicist (sportsethicist.com), a blog and podcast in which he discusses the philosophical and ethical issues in and around sport. He edits the book series, *Studies in the Philosophy of Sport*. He has fond memories of his Apple IIe, but truly could not live without his iPhone and iPad.

DENNIS KNEPP teaches philosophy and religious studies at Big Bend Community College in Moses Lake, Washington. He has previously published essays applying philosophy to *Twilight*, *Alice in Wonderland*, *The Hobbit*, *The Girl with the Dragon Tattoo*, *Superman*, *Black Sabbath*, and *Avatar*. His first Apple was a 1993 Christmas present (thanks, Mom and Dad!): a Macintosh Color Classic which he employed to finish his bachelor's degree at Wichita State University, using it exclusively all through graduate school at Washington University in St. Louis, and even finished his dissertation with it in 2001. Currently in his home there are four iPhones, three iPods, two MacBooks, and a 2009 24-inch iMac in need of replacement.

RYAN KRAUSE is Assistant Professor of Strategy in the Neeley School of Business at Texas Christian University. He received his PhD in strategic management and organization theory from Indiana University. Ryan conducts research primarily on issues relating to corporate governance, including boards of directors, executive succession, and stakeholder management. His work has appeared in the *Academy of Management Journal, Academy of Management Review, Strategic Management Journal,* and *Journal of Management.* His research has also been covered in the popular business press, in outlets such as the *Wall Street Journal, New York Times, USA Today, Fortune, Businessweek,* and Fox Business Network. Use of any and all Apple products is encouraged in his classroom, so long as it causes students to Think Different.

JAMES EDWIN MAHON is Professor of Philosophy and Chair of the Department of Philosophy at Washington and Lee University. His main research interests are in moral philosophy and in early modern philosophy. When he first moved to W&L in 2000 he was one of only a few Mac users on campus, and he experienced discrimination; now Macs outnumber PCs among faculty and students, and he is having the last laugh.

JARED MEYER is a fellow at the Manhattan Institute. He is a graduate of St. John's University where he received a BS in finance and a minor in the philosophy of law. Jared's research interests include microeconomic theory and the motivations for, along with the economic effects of, governmental regulations. He was previously a research assistant for the political philosopher Douglas Rasmussen, and Jared continues to publish and present on the need for a moral foundation of free markets. Jared is still upset that, as a four-year-old, his parents refused his request to let him change his name to Woody (after the star of Steve Jobs's first movie with Pixar Studios, *Toy Story*).

KYLE MUNKITTRICK thinks his iPhone is literally a part of his brain and treats it as such. He first realized he was using cybernetics "designed in California" while earning his MA in Bioethics and Human Enhancement from New York University (while working at an Apple store, mind you). Since then he's written about bioethics, pop culture, and the future of humanity all over the internet. Kyle is currently trying to fix the healthcare industry from the inside out. He's optimistic about Apple creating something like a tricorder and that Pixar will do the right thing and finally make a sequel to *The Incredibles*.

TERRY W. NOEL is Associate Professor of Management and Quantitative Methods at Illinois State University where he teaches classes in both Entrepreneurship and Management. Dr. Noel's work has been published in such places as the *Academy of Management Journal*, the *Journal of Management Education*, and the *Journal of Entrepreneurship Education*. His research focuses on the process of entrepreneurial learning and how entrepreneurial thinking can benefit both startups and established organizations. He recently purchased his first iPhone and would marry it if Illinois law allowed.

PAUL PARDI is adjunct professor of philosophy at Seattle Pacific University and publisher of the popular philosophy blog philosophynews.com. His main philosophical interests focus on epistemology, philosophy of religion, and anything having to do with the intersection between philosophy and culture. He's also a Senior Content Development Manager at Microsoft where Steve Jobs's products and industry influence has kept him on his toes (and generated enough hard work to keep him employed) for the last fifteen years.

OWEN PARKER is is an assistant professor of management in the Spears School of Business at Oklahoma State University. He received his PhD from the Kelley School of Business at Indiana University. His research primarily focuses on the influence of reputation dynamics on product novelty and introduction speed, and has been featured in the Best Paper Proceedings of the Academy of Management. Whether reading iBooks or playing Angry Birds, he always has his iPhone at hand.

ROBERT F. SALVINO is Associate Professor of Economics at Coastal Carolina University. He teaches advanced courses in economics and entrepreneurship, and his research examines the effects of government rules and institutions on economic outcomes. A couple of students triggered his interest in Steve Jobs. One student was a Mac guy who kept recommending the switch from a PC in order to create cartoons or movies to better explain economic concepts. A second student noted how similar Jobs seemed compared to Ayn Rand characters. That was enough. Salvino bought Isaacson's biography of Steve Jobs in a coffee shop the next day, the day it was released.

WILLIAM R THOMAS is Director of Programs at The Atlas Society and is a sometime lecturer in economics at the University at Albany. He is the editor of *The Literary Art of Ayn Rand* and the author of many essays and book reviews. His research interests focus on developing social ethics from an Objectivist perspective. He is the only person he knows who could not figure out easily how to use an iPod scroll wheel, but Steve Jobs finally won him over with the iPad.

JASON WALKER currently lives in Beijing, holding a dual appointment as an assistant professor at Renmin University's School of Philosophy, and as a lecturer at China Foreign Affairs University. Although he grew up using an Apple IIGS, Jason has owned no Apple products since 1996. His current laptop is a Gateway running Windows 7, his tablet of choice (which he used to write most of his chapter) is a Nook HD+, and he still listens to most of his music on a Zune 120. His phone is a ZTE Android "pseudo-intellectual" phone, but he hopes to get a decent Android smart phone when he returns to the US. He thinks Apple products are just fine, merely a bit overpriced and overrated.

ROBERT WHITE is an assistant professor of philosophy and Chair of the Department of Business at the American University in Bulgaria, where he teaches business ethics. His PhD on

Ayn Rand's ethics was completed at the University of Auckland, New Zealand, and was written on the original iMac. Today, he uses a MacBook Pro at home, a MacBook Air in the office and classroom, reads magazines and books on an iPad, and watches movies on AppleTV. He looks forward to replacing his cardio sports watch with an AppleWatch. He is pleased that his newborn son will live in a world forever touched by the mind of Steve Jobs.

There's a Page for That!

237

bad faith, 168–69
Bailey, George, 16
Barber, Benjamin, 18
Bauhaus, 200
*Be the Solution: How
    Entrepreneurs and
    Conscious Capitalists Can
    Solve All the World's
    Problems* (Strong), 21
Being and Nothingness (Sartre),
    217
Being and Time (Heidegger),
    183, 216
Bell, Alexander Graham, 77,
    92–93
Bentham, Jeremy, 101, 212–13
benevolence, 10, 102–03, 110
Big Brother, 11, 15, 87
Binswanger, Harry, 133, 135
Bono (U2), 100
brains, 41–42, 157, 234
Brave, 43. *See also* Pixar
Breakout, 8
Brennan, Chrisann (Jobs's
    ex–girlfriend), 9
Brennan, Lisa (Jobs's daughter),
    9, 107, 199
The Brothers Karamazov
    (Dostoyevsky), 166
Buddha, 36, 114–16, 123, 207.
    See also Buddhism
Buddhism, 22, 36, 113–125, 140,
    200, 207
Buffett, Warren, 76, 88, 99
The Bug's Life, 43, 44. *See also*
    Pixar

Callas, Maria, 128, 135
Campbell, Joseph, 35
cancer, 10, 15, 132,
capitalism, xii, 15–22, 25, 57, 68,
    70, 78, 80–82, 84, 214, 216
Cars, 43, 122, 144. *See also* Pixar

Categorical Imperative, 104, 139,
    212. *See also* Kant,
    Immanuel
cell phone, xii, 96, 191
charity, 73, 99, 100–111, 151,
    153. *See also* philanthropy
China, 41, 74, 75, 235
Chinese Room thought-
    experiment, 41, 42, 218. *See
    also* Searle, John
A Christmas Carol (Dickens), 17
Churchland, Paul, 156
citizenship, 33, 39, 74, 231
Coleman, Deb, 6, 11
competition, 17, 65, 72, 178–181
computer animation, 90. *See also*
    Pixar
Confucianism, 34
consciousness, 21, 39–40, 78,
    116–17, 121–22, 131–34,
    181, 217–19. *See also* mind
Cook, Tim, 31, 149, 152
Corning Glass, 133–34
corporations, 72, 92, 99, 145, 149,
    151–160
Corporate Moral Agency (CMA),
    151–161
Cote, Judge Denise, 173–79
counter-culture, xii, 15–19,
    20–25, 199
courage, 20–21, 27, 31, 47, 58,
    61–63, 70, 103, 142
creativity, 16, 21–22, 24, 30, 32,
    35, 54–57, 61–62, 65–66,
    69–70, 111, 138, 140, 199,
    216–17
creative destruction, 69, 70, 216.
    See also Schumpeter, Joseph
    A.
creator, 8, 31, 35Cronkite, Walter,
    183–86, 190–93
Csikszentmihalyi, Mihaly, 21
Cue, Eddy, 174–78, 182
Curie, Marie, 110